Is This Really You?

An environmentally friendly book printed and bound in England by
www.printondemand-worldwide.com

This book is made entirely of chain-of-custody materials

Is This Really You?

Understanding Who You Are
and Where You're Going

Trisha Alleyne

www.fast-print.net/store.php

Is This Really You?

Copyright © Trisha Alleyne 2013

All rights reserved

A catalogue record for this book is available from the British Library

ISBN 978-178035-584-9

The right of Trisha Alleyne to be identified as the author of this work has been asserted by her in accordance with the Copyright, Designs and Patents Act 1988 and any subsequent amendments thereto.

This is a work of fact inspired by true life events. Nevertheless, some names of people and places have been changed to protect the privacy of the individuals concerned.

No part of this book may be reproduced in any form by photocopying or any electronic or mechanical means, including information storage or retrieval systems, without permission in writing from both the copyright owner and the publisher of the book.

About The Author

Trisha Alleyne is a former senior housing officer, wife and mother of four. She began writing a diary in 2004 as a form of therapy, until with gentle encouragement from her daughter, who was amazed by the challenges she faced throughout her life, she went on to tell her whole dramatic story in the form of a trilogy. This book forms the first part.

Born in 1966, Trisha grew up in North West London where she spent many years moving around, trying desperately to find somewhere to call home, before eventually settling in Kent. She is currently attending university, studying for a degree in Business Management.

Acknowledgements

My first Thank you, is to God, the Lord most high. I thank you for carrying me when I felt I could no longer continue through life's journey. Thank you for giving me the strength, the faith and the conviction to pursue the changes that I needed to make.

To my two eldest children

Ishmel Alleyne and Isharna Alleyne I thank you for understanding and knowing who you are and where you're going and showing me what I needed to do to establish peace, happiness and contentment in my life.

To my two younger children

Ricardo Alleyne and Reeo-Jay Alleyne. I thank you both for just being you.

To my mother

I want you to know that I understand and accept that you raised and did the best for me you possibly could. I hold no ill feelings towards you. I want you to know that I respect you and still admire you as the most elegant and graceful focused black woman that I have ever known.

Love you mum

To Brother Lincoln

I thank you for all the help and guidance you gave me throughout my twenty-year quest to find religion. Because of you I became strong in my faith and my beliefs.

To Laura

You were the first friend to whom I read a small extract of this book. You encouraged me and cemented my belief that I had written something worth publishing. I thank you.

To my wonderful husband

My rock, the man that has anchored himself at my side and allowed me to cry, to heal, to tell my story my soul mate, I thank you from the bottom of my heart.

This book is dedicated to all of you.

Contents

‘Is This Really You?’

An Inspiring True Story
of Self-Discovery

By Trisha …

Part One

The Journey Begins

In this the first volume of her autobiographical trilogy, Trisha reveals the heart-rending difficulties and dilemmas of growing up in a domineering and dysfunctional family. Ridiculed, exploited and violently abused by vindictive, bullying siblings, Pat (her then name) finds it a struggle simply to survive, let alone make any sense of her life. Discovering in her teens an uncanny gift for clairvoyance further unsettles her, and those around her.

Desperate to break free from the torments of her past and escape the negative cycle of her existence, she leaves home, striving to build her confidence and create an independent life of her own. But neither the past, nor her family, will let her alone. Will she ever find the strength, acceptance and happiness – not to mention love in the shape of Mr Right – for which she so ardently yearns? And will 'Pat' ever throw off the shackles of her former self to become the confident, successful and fulfilled 'Trisha'?

Chapter One

Is This Really You?

We have arrived and finally, the removal men have gone. It feels like they've been here all day; the many empty rum and coke bottles and plates of half eaten flying fish and chicken wings litter the patio table. Reggae music blares out courtesy of my eldest son Isaac, our own resident DJ. His tall, slim physique and coffee coloured skin darkened by two shades in the sun, overpowered by the enormous headphones he uses to mix and scratch the music, he is in his element. While the children run around in T-shirts and shorts playing with their water guns, the scorching rays of the sun beat down. The atmosphere is full of joy and laughter. I hear Ricky's voice. Ricky is my husband, my strength, my rock, my conscience. Who would have thought I would end up married to someone so wonderful like him, with his strong, solid, tall, dark-skinned and of course handsome self. From the day he walked into my life he anchored himself to my side and there he is happy to stay as my soul mate. He is calling to our high-spirited, water-fighting sons: 'Skipper!' he shouts, his Barbadian accent back with a vengeance, 'wheeait..! 'Dis furniture come all de way from England to Barbados, good-good, onenah please d-hon't come and mash it up now wid' onenah waatar – mine, onenah don't get it wet.'

'Don't worry Dad,' Ilana pipes up in a rather sarcastic, sweetie-pie voice.' Sun-kissed skin, legs up to her armpits she gives a flick of her free flowing, naturally spiralling curls. 'This is Barbados – it will dry in no time.' Repositioning herself back on the sun lounger, this beauty that I have created, my daughter. Sculpted to near perfection, she rolls over to allow even tanning of her 5 foot 8 inch frame, scantly covered by an array of colour in three small triangles, and replaces her sunglasses. Is this the body of a future top model?

Leaving them outside, my perfect family to it, I went upstairs to what was now my new bedroom. I looked around my gleaming white en-suite bathroom and walk-in wardrobe, the clean whitewashed walls and gleaming varnished floor. It was 2006 and I was the proud owner of the most gorgeous four-bedroom house on the block. A real dream come true. I never thought that we would really make it. But Ricky was confident and convincing, always assuring me, 'Trisha if anyone can, you can. I know we can make this dream of ours a reality. Just imagine after 17 years of asking your mum for a piece of her land at the bottom of her garden in Barbados, there was always an obstacle, some sort of problem, but I have no fears or doubts that with your determination, we will be able to achieve this on our own, without the help of anyone.'

I stood at the entrance of the yet to be furnished room surrounded by boxes, black bags and huge storage containers filled with possessions and trinkets that seemed to jingle within, reminding me, whispering their presence. I wondered if I would ever find homes for all these beautiful things. As I started to unpack the first box, I cautiously peeled back the bubble wrap that housed an antique Victorian style framed looking glass, carefully handling this fragile object that had weathered the storms of yesteryear. I sat quietly. A glimpse of myself in this mirror reminded me of where I had come from and where I was today. It held my secrets, and the mysteries of my life. It's funny, the things you buy and the things you keep that stay with you throughout your life. A simple mirror that I had bought so many years ago had travelled the length and breadth of the UK with me, and now across the Atlantic Ocean. I took a long hard look at myself again. 'Trisha,' I said to myself, 'Is this really you?'

Sitting down on a box, I stared closer into the mirror, studying my reflection. I thought: who is this person? Suddenly the feelings of relief, happiness and contentment I had been enjoying began to distort and dissolve; now in their place came anger, confusion and distress, as dreadful thoughts of the past rose up to haunt me. Desperately I closed my eyes, blinked hard and tried to force these memories away, but as always it was no good. The past, my own mind, why could I not command them? I wanted to cry. Yet again, I needed the tears to wash away my unwelcome thoughts.

I allowed my mind to drift, to travel back to a place and time when things were very different, when I was Pat. Let the memories come, let the tears flow. For now was the time for healing to take place. It was 1974, and I saw myself. I was Pat…

Pat was wearing the red coat that her mum bought her on her 8th birthday. Pat's mum was putting the red coat on her. 'Pat, when I saw this coat, I had to buy it for you as you're my Little Red Riding Hood. You're kind, loving and sweet, and always willing to do for others …' Before she could finish her sentence, Pat jumped in and said, 'But Mum, the Wolf ate Little Red Riding Hood, is someone going to eat me?'

'What nonsense Pat, replied Mum. 'What are you talking about child?' When Mum had finished fastening the buttons Pat ran upstairs to her sisters. Hers was a big family. Suzette the eldest of the girls was born in Barbados and raised till she was eight years old on the beautiful island of Dominica by her grandparents, Nana Mar Christina and Granddad Par Dubois. They were regarded there as aristocrats by their farming neighbours, though as country bumpkins by the town folk.

Suzette was a quiet, withdrawn child, and very much the loner. There will be more to say about her, but later. Karman, the first of the O'Neal tribe, born here in the UK, came next. She too was quiet and reserved but had brains and beauty too.

Marianne was Pat's baby sister and her most treasured possession. Mum placed her in Pat's arms the day they returned home from hospital. 'This is your baby,' she had told Pat. 'You must love her, care for her and protect her.' These words Pat had embedded in her heart, and she would strive to carry them out for the next twenty years, until Pat reached a point in her life when she said, enough was enough.

Pat wore her new red coat the whole day, being careful not to get it dirty and living up to her Little Red Riding Hood reputation. As helpful as Pat would try to be however, the frosty feelings that blew from sister to sister towards her did not go unnoticed.

Every day, for Pat 7.30 pm couldn't come soon enough. That was when her dad and two older brothers came home from work. Her dad, a small, short slip of a man with his shiny black skin and small shaven head was a well-educated person, and very strict. But Pat knew his bark was worst than his bite.

Dad was raised back home in the upper class area of town, among the elite and the wealthy. After serving as a policeman in Dominica for many years he now worked for London Transport.

Pat's family lived in Basildon, a new town in the countryside, which meant they didn't get to see a great deal of Dad during the week, though more at weekends, mainly Sundays. To Pat though, he was the best dad in the world. The two of them had a great relationship, despite his strict demeanour. He had a wonderful sense of humour and was quite the party animal – singing and dancing and playing loud music on Sundays, urging his children to take turns learning the dance routines of years gone by, like the waltz, foxtrot and quickstep, and not forgetting the rhythms of sweet reggae and calypso music from back home. Dancing remained Dad's passion, albeit in the privacy of his home.

Pat's big brother Roger, the eldest of the O'Neal tribe, born in Dominica, was small and short just like Dad, but of lighter complexion. He was the joker of the family, always laughing and smiling, never taking things too seriously. Her other brother, Ronald, also having Dad's shiny dark skin and small, short physique, was a completely opposite personality to Roger. Ronald was extremely serious, forever the pessimist, so serious in fact that he would only joke and laugh on special occasions.

On the whole the O'Neal tribe was a close knit one, so Pat thought. They were a family that thrived on love and mutual support, borne through their mum. At night Mum would let down her mane of shoulder length, full bodied cocoa brown hair and her daughters would fuss over taking turns to brush it, against her flawless latte coloured skin. Mum was the picture of beauty in Pat's eyes, the most graceful and elegant woman she'd ever met. Mother, with her calm voice, loving smile and tender touch, was the real driving force in the family.

Although not educated beyond the age of eleven, not that anyone would believe it, she carried herself and raised her children as if she had been to one of Switzerland's most exclusive finishing schools for the rich and famous. As the eldest of sixteen children, the burden of helping to raise them had fallen on her shoulders. 'Mum was the one' Pat thought, who held everything and everyone together. Only gradually and painfully, did she come to realise that the family values her mother had preached to her were not always even handed or just, and could be twisted and distorted with depressing, devastating consequences.

Pat's childhood in Basildon was one of very mixed emotions. In between interludes of happiness she felt a silent anger, pain and despair. She spent many nights alone wondering why she felt so different – different from her sisters. When her parents weren't around she occupied herself with music and dancing to avoid being the target of their repeated 'ugly' jokes. Dancing to her favourite songs she would front a smile as the music played, but deep down inside she was hurting. 'Why, why, why?' she asked herself again and again, 'do they keep on doing this to me? Am I really that ugly?' Like most children, as Pat grew, she had become aware of her appearance, curious about it, sensitive to how she looked. She would peer in the mirror with a sense of trepidation and dread, uncertain about the image that stared back at her – was her face a pleasant one, nice, or even just what a 'normal' girl's face was supposed to look like? Or was she as weird, freakish or plain old ugly as her sisters repeatedly told her? She feared they must be right. The name-calling was a ritual led by Suzette: 'ugly, ugly, ugly…' while encouraging the others at every opportunity to join in.

It might then seem strange that entering the teenage years, although the 'ugly' taunts didn't stop, Pat and Suzette became very close. Pat looked up to Suzette and admired her as she developed into an astute and a focused black woman, very much like their mother. It was just after Pat's boring 15th birthday that Suzette announced to the family she was getting married to Ivan, the father of her son Marlo. Pat was truly excited, knowing in her heart she would have a huge part to play in this wedding, planned for July 15th 1982. The whole family pulled together and did their bit to make this much-anticipated event a joyous occasion, Suzette being the first born daughter, and the first to get married. Their sister Karman meanwhile was now pregnant with her first child, and though unable to do much was just as excited as the rest of the family. Pat was thrilled too at the prospect of having a little niece or nephew.

Pat was requested to be Suzette's chief bridesmaid, a responsibility she accepted happily. She helped organise the other four bridesmaids, and for the first time ever felt in seventh heaven, able to show off her organisational skills, budgeting and planning abilities, her flair for fashion and design, and imagination in coming up with ideas, while always mindful not to overstep the mark. She suggested the colours for the bridesmaids, their dress designs and accessories, right down to their shoes and hairstyles.

This was the biggest event the O'Neal tribe had ever had to organise, and of course, it had to be, not only the biggest, but also the best wedding any of the guests had ever been to. Mum and Dad didn't spare a thought for the financial outlay – we don't care what it costs, we must have it – was their attitude. You would think Suzette was their only child. A horse and carriage was to convey the bride and her father to the church, and at the reception, guests would partake of a lavish a-la-carte, sit-down meal with waitress service. As for the cake, well, it was a case of 'not what you know, but who you know' and Suzette's was to be designed and created by the prestigious 'Classic Celebration Cakes' of Cheshire, a firm that had been involved in supplying cakes for the previous five official royal weddings, including Lady Diana's. All the men were to wear top hat and tails, with gleaming Roll Royce wedding cars laid on for immediate family, and a fleet of six Mercedes to collect close friends. The guest list was soon numbering five hundred. Wow! What a wedding this was going to be!

As the big day drew nearer and nearer, with only the minor things left to do, Pat started to notice cracks in the family's unity. It was as if things were only fine when it suited specific members, and if it didn't, well there would be a cold chill in the air. Pat couldn't quite understand any of these issues at the time, but sensed that a day would come when she would, and would have to accept and deal with the division that was causing pain in her heart and tears in her eyes.

Meanwhile, Pat was to have an unsettling experience. She was not afraid of the beautiful ebony skinned lady that one night appeared to her in a vision. The figure had not glowed, as most people tend to think angels do. No, she had looked just like you and I, except for a sweet smell of lavender that followed her. She showed Pat pictures of the bedroom the family had decorated for Karman and her baby's arrival home. There was a banner she and her younger sisters had painted: 'Welcome home Karman and Baby.' Flowers were arranged lovingly around the bedroom and of course, there was the blue silk canopy, which Mum had made for the cot. Perfect, Pat thought, just perfect. Until that is, the lady showed her pictures of an empty cot. What did it mean? Pat wondered -flowers, banner, canopy, Karman – but no baby?

The same vision returned to Pat many times during Karman's pregnancy. The week the baby was due it came again. This time she decided to tell her mother. Her mother was horrified. She saw her own duty clearly: to put a stop to whatever it was that had got into her daughter. Without stopping to even consider what it might mean, or giving an explanation, she lashed out. The blow struck Pat's left cheek, sending the back of her head smashing against the wall. It was accompanied by a barrage of abuse that left no doubt what her mother thought of her; she was wicked, evil, a child of the devil, who had no good intentions for her sister or her unborn nephew.

A few days later in early December Karman went into labour; more excitement for the O'Neal's. The baby boy was born and named Edmund. But the joyfulness was very short lived. Karman's baby died at just nine days old, before even coming home. It threw the whole family into depression. For Pat, the struggle was to come to terms not only with the loss of her nephew, but also what she had experienced prior the tragic event. Edmund never saw the flowers, the banner, or the blue silk canopy that his grandmother had made. It was just as the lady in her vision had shown her.

Around this time everyone at school was planning their sweet 16th birthday bashes, and Pat was having secret bashes with herself yet again, convincing herself she had done all she could to change the minds of her mother and sister to rethink the date of baby Edmund's funeral. Despite all the tears she cried, all the begging and pleading – 'make it the day before, or the day after, please…' it made no difference to them. Baby Edmund was buried on the 21st December 1982, Pats 16th birthday. How wicked was that? Pat was dismissed and led to believe this was not about her. 'In any case, what's the big deal?' was her mother's response. 'Your birthday is so near to Christmas we don't celebrate it anyway.'

While the family were still coming to terms with the loss of baby Edmund, his funeral had taken place. Things started to get back on track, though a very different light shone on the arrangements for Suzette's wedding. Pat was called aside by Suzette and asked if she would now mind if Karman could be chief bridesmaid, to help take her mind off the death of her son. Suzette told Pat how sorry she was, as she knew how much she was looking forward to playing her part on the big day. Pat certainly felt the disappointment running through her, but understood and agreed, saying she didn't mind as she too felt this would help Karman. Karman accepted the role as chief bridesmaid, and whilst Pat tried hard to be helpful still, and involved in the final preparations, she found herself increasingly left out and no longer wanted around.

It was three weeks before the big day when Karman dropped a bombshell on Suzette. She announced she was pregnant again and now no longer wanted to be a bridesmaid. Suzette was thrown into turmoil and didn't know what to do, other than come back to Pat and ask her to step back in. In fact, she demanded it. Before Pat could respond, her mother weighed in: 'I know you feel that we have left you out over the past few months, and it's a bit of a cheek for us to ask you this, but it's an emergency so please just paint that beautiful smile on your face and say yes you'll do it.' Pat felt she had no choice.

The wedding went off like a military operation, from start to finish everything was perfectly timed and in place. The bride looked beautiful, bridesmaids and flower girls looked beautiful, the groom handsome as could be. The big grand wedding of the year, it was great. So why did Pat feel so strange? She had worked hard in the last few weeks to pull everything together, and her job as chief bridesmaid had been well done everyone said so – so why the uncomfortable feelings inside? Perhaps she was looking for that special pat on the back, the genuine, personal thank you, any sign of real appreciation. But they were not forthcoming.

Over the next couple of years the distance between Pat and her sisters grew wider and deeper. They had nothing in common; she was the dumb, ugly duckling, the black sheep of the family – loud, boisterous, with more male than female friends, and she loved music and dancing -the complete opposite of her sisters. So, Pat isolated herself, kept away from them, and pushed herself into her dancing. At the dance studio, in the big mirrors, she began to see in her reflection a different person, one who could conjure exciting, eloquent shapes, whose artistry and skills tapped the rich resource of her natural gift to pour forth a whole new language, capable of communicating beyond the power of words, expressing an array of rich feelings – melancholy and joy, laughter, curiosity, enchantment. Pat enrolled on a course, and strived towards a future career in dance. Neither of her parents took this at all seriously. Her mother felt that she was wasting her time and that she should find a worthwhile profession such as nursing, that she simply wasn't good enough to make it as a dancer. Never did she utter a word of encouragement or say anything positive about her daughter's ambition. Finally though, under duress, she did turn up with Suzette to Pat's final dance performance at college. It was then that she was told by Pat's teacher, 'Mrs O'Neal, your daughter has such raw natural talent; it's been a long time since I have seen someone with this kind of passion and ability, that hasn't been trained. With the right kind of teaching she could go very far.'

Pat was not really sure how much of an impact hearing those words from her teacher made on her mother, as she showed little change in her attitude. She did assist Pat with paying for her dance classes, but only when it suited her. The purchase of anything else to do with dancing was non-existent. This Pat could live with, as she understood it was not what her mum had in mind for her daughter. But it seemed a crying shame that Dad, the one who had introduced his family to music and dance, the person who at eighteen had won a scholarship to the world renowned Dance Academy in Guadalupe, showed no real interest either. It just added to Pat's frustration and sense of feeling misunderstood. Here we go again, thought Pat, same thing – different day; she was angry, furious again, but silently. Confused as always, she wanted the world to know, but with no idea how to communicate these feelings. In constant fear of her emotions, and living solely to keep on the right side of those whom she thought loved her, was a full-time job. With her fondest hopes, to become a dancer, ignored by her family, neglect and self-doubt became a habit.

* * * * * *

Pat was the part of me that quite simply refused to change, she refused to grow, and she was the part of me that needed healing. The part where all of my fears and character flaws were hidden; this was not about having a split personality, it was about Pat's history.

Trisha was creating her own history. Pat had a history, of pain, abuse and neglect; she had a history of doing things in a certain way with certain expectations, which were all based on painful experiences. A lot of these experiences often allowed her to neglect herself, her own needs, in the pursuit of the approval and acceptance of her family. I understood Pat's history and her submissive behaviour towards her family, but I also understood and knew I had the power to change.

Me, Trisha, believed with a passion that I had the right to live in peace, and that I had the ability to transform my way of thinking and being, to become the person I wanted to be, a complete human being. I knew to achieve this I would have to merge what I used to be with what I could be and want to be – Pat and Trisha had to become one. But could it be done?

* * * * * *

At eighteen Pat left home and moved to the other side of London. She visited Mum and Dad, and the younger members of the family that were still at home as often as possible and continued her education in performing arts. I guess this was a happy time for Pat, as she shared a house with three other girls, and finally felt wanted and needed by others. She cooked the Sunday lunch for her is housemates and their partners, she washed and cleaned and felt appreciated for the first time in her life. No 'ugly' jokes, no teasing, no belittling. In fact they loved her!! It all started to make sense for Pat, as she understood that changes needed to be made in her life, and accepted that even when these changes were made, her history would not change. For what you learn through your experiences, will influence and motivate everything you do during the rest of your life.

It was one bright summer's day, early evening in fact, while Pat relaxed in the garden that a vision came to her. It was not like before, the beautiful ebony skinned lady did not appear to her. But Pat could feel her presence, and could smell the soothing aroma of lavender. She saw a cartoon drawing of a desert island – you know the kind of thing, the little funny shaped bit of land, one palm tree in the middle, surrounded by water? Yeah, that's the one! There was water, water, and more water. This was the first of many times that Pat would see this vision. Each time it appeared the image would remain with her a little bit longer, but the theme remained the same, a small island with lots of water. Then she saw something else; her mum crying, and a plane landing on the cartoon island, and this time her beautiful, ebony skinned lady was there again, appearing in a variety of different female guises.

Pat felt compelled to say something, but what? She had never forgotten the reaction she got from her mother when she told her about the vision of baby Edmund; how on earth could she tell her now she felt something was wrong back home in Dominica, and that this beautiful ebony skinned lady she had been seeing in her dreams was in fact Nana Mar Christina? How could she convey to her mum that she needed to get to Dominica as soon as possible? With all the courage and strength that Pat could muster, she told her mum about the vision, and of course it was taken the wrong way completely.

'Why do you do that?' demanded her mum. 'Are you not old enough to find something constructive to do with yourself, rather than going around upsetting people with your nonsense.'

'It's not nonsense Mum,' insisted Pat. 'There is something wrong with Nanna Christina.' Pat sobbed.

Weeks passed and the visions kept on coming, more intense and powerful than before. Pat felt duty-bound, forced even, to insist that the least her mum should do was call back home to Dominica, to ensure everything was okay. During the time it took for her mum to come to terms with what Pat had said and actually make the phone call, Nana Mar Christina had been diagnosed and was dying of cancer.

The last vision that had appeared concerning Nana Mar Christina had been more like a warning to Pat; the series of women the ebony skinned woman had illustrated for her were all strong black women – Mary Seacole; a born healer, a woman of driving energy, she had overcome prejudice and the indifference of bureaucracy to help the injured and dying during The Crimean War of 18531856, a contemporary who achieved at least as much as Florence Nightingale. Pat had also seen Sojourner Truth, a women's rights activist and abolitionist of the 1800s, remembered for her famous speech, 'Ain't I a woman?' in 1851 at the Ohio Women's Rights Convention. Shirley Chisholm also appeared; the first African-American woman elected to the U.S. Congress, who had hired an all-female staff to show her dedication to advocating for women. Also Madam C.J. Parker, an inspiring entrepreneur who created a complete range of hair care products for black women, which sold throughout the country. What did it mean? Why was Pat shown these women in her visions?

Only after her mother waited and waited for her sister to get her act together to go to Dominica to hopefully see their mother before she closed her eyes for the last time, did Pat realise and understand. They were too late. Nanna Mar Christina passed away before they got to her.

When her mother returned to the UK she was broken. Pat had never seen this strong, focused, independent woman like this before. She seemed shattered into so many pieces, weak and off-balance. How, wondered Pat, should she respond?

* * * * * *

Unconditional love, which family life should exemplify, does not mean that you accept or condone mistreatment. But it does require that you excuse people for their faults and frailties; that you see them, accept them and love them for who they are, regardless of the things you may or may not like about them.

* * * * * *

Pat's vision, of strong, courageous black women had shown her that in her own, immediate world she too had to do the right thing – the dutiful thing, which right then, was to accept and try to help her mother.

Chapter Two
Love at First Sight

It was the summer of '84. Pat was still being Pat, angry, silently angry, anxious, naïve and simple minded in affairs of the heart. Her flatmates spoke openly of their relationships, problems and aspirations, something quite unfamiliar to Pat. She began to feel like the odd one out, and though her focus was primarily on her dancing and creating a career for herself, she secretly desired the warmth, the comfort and the security of a loving relationship, where she would be the centre of attention, she would be the queen. She would be like her friends staying out late, wined and dined and treated like she was the most important person in the world.

Nearby Pat's place of work they were trying out for the local men's body building competition, hundreds of them, mini power houses, flexing and posing, walking around like they had already won the title of Mr Universe. Yeah right! As Pat walked around in her Pineapple Studios leotard and tights, the fashion statement of every professional dancer (wannabe), she giggled secretly to herself. She was mesmerized not only by the fantastic physiques, and the display of so much exposed male flesh and testosterone flowing in abundance, but more so by the fact that she had never encountered any male that was so focused and so dedicated to creating a successful future. She was in awe of this whole new experience.

Wow! And there he was, stood in nothing but spandex briefs, oiled from head to toe, perfecting his routine of stretches, flexes and poses. Pat's jaw dropped to the floor, palms sweating and heart pounding loud enough to hear it in her ears. Their eyes met. She gasped, and was suddenly immobile. Shit! Fix up! Look sharp! Sort it out! With those words echoing in her mind, she quickly fixed up her leotard, pulled up her tights, patted her weave, moistened her pouted lips and arched her back to accentuate her inherited Afro-Caribbean, Coca Cola bottle shaped figure. That was it; Pat thought she was in love. The cliché love at first sight comes to mind. She thought this was it!

Pat was not disappointed. The dream guy's name was Ray, he was 6ft 2in tall, had caramel coloured skin, dreamy brown eyes, and a physique that sent her pulse racing. Before she knew it they were on a date. When he took her in his powerful arms to dance, she felt so on fire that she thought she might melt. Their first kiss was electrifying, and as they said goodnight, and Ray said, 'I'll call you,' she felt she was on cloud nine, at least. Cloud ten was when he kept the promise. She was so nervous she could hardly hold the phone steady. Soon it was bedtime, not that either of them got much sleep. Ray was a fantastic lover, immensely masculine, passionate – sensual but dominant, his powerful manhood entering Pat and sweeping her to heights of pleasure she had never known were possible. It happened again, and again and again, the two of them drunk on each other's vivacious young bodies. In between Ray showered her with gifts – cheap gifts, market brought perfume, non-name brand clothes, knocked off jewellery, and oh yeah the flowers, what a joke. But Pat thought she had died and gone to heaven.

Along with the intense passion there followed a strange time that Pat spent with Ray, full of mixed emotions, wistful feelings, joys and disappointments. Pat's initial thoughts, like most other teenage girls, was that this would be the love of her life, the man that would take her to great heights, that would share in all of her dreams and aspirations, make her feel whole and treat her like the Queen she believed she should be. But was Ray ready for a commitment, ready to settle down and appreciate a woman, a wife, a Queen, as well as take on the emotional baggage that came with Pat?

Ray was certainly independent, and liked to go out on his own, but if this was a problem, perhaps Pat could deal with it. Despite all the upsets, all the heartaches, all the sleepless lonely nights, she sat back watching her friends with their partners going out partying, enjoying themselves in each other's company, whilst she was being left at home. But Pat felt she had made a commitment to Ray and was prepared to accept whatever he put her through.

The thing was, Pat had lived a life where she acknowledged and was well aware that love hurt, so the expectation of love with no pain was incomprehensible to her. The mirror image of her parents' marital relationship was being reflected; Mum and Dad had never shown any love towards one another, no physical contact, no displays of affection and appreciation of each other. Was there ever any chemistry between them?

It was a situation where Pat tried desperately to push aside what she had grown up with and the limited knowledge she had of relationships, based on her parents, versus what she now saw as a good relationship based around her friends. Although what she saw and heard about her friends and their relationships was enviable, Pat put that aside and stayed with what she knew and had experienced from a distance – accepting a so-so, loveless, emotionless, stale, cold, stagnant relationship, just like her parents. If this was as good as it got, maybe that was OK.

Ray hadn't been round for a few days. Pat accepted this as the norm. It was late in the afternoon when he finally turned up. Surprisingly not with the usual bunch of half dead daffodils that he had picked from somebody's garden, or even the half eaten bar of chocolate he would normally bring to her as a token of his love, which Pat gladly accepted. 'We need to talk,' he said, but there was no emotion in his voice, just his usual calm self. Thoughts of a night out whisked through Pat's mind: I'm in for a treat, as my favourite reggae artist Beres Hammond is performing in town. It's been a long time since we went out together, looks like we are actually going to do the couple thing – you know what I mean, get dressed up, heels, makeup, oh my gosh I need to do my hair! Finally the girls will have the opportunity to beautify me. Wow! Makes a change as it's always me beautifying them… Then Ray spoke again: 'It's just not working out.'

'What do you mean it's not working out?'

'I can't take the stress, you obviously have a lot of issues that need to be dealt with and I'm sorry, I ain't got the time, nor the patience to deal with you.'

Tears filled Pat's eyes. 'Yeah, the sex is great, but that's all that's great.' On his way out the front door he turned and said, 'You still look good; yeah man you know you still look good! Body fit! Any man will pick you up; you know how to work it. Later, yeah.'

Pat was heartbroken, the man she fell in love with at first sight had just walked out of her life.

Days turned into weeks, and weeks into months, Pat finally began to get over the breakup of her and Ray and vowed that she would never be used by any man ever again. Sex was something she decided was dirty and unclean and was used as a form of punishment for all her shortcomings and failures as a worthy girlfriend. The words 'the sex was good, but that's all that was good' replayed over and over in her mind, bringing her to the conclusion that sex was all she was good for; if the man she loved could say this to her, then it must be true. For Pat sex was now obsolete. For two years of her life she had stayed in this relationship, just for him to walk out on her, how could this be?

A relationship of sorts had formed between Pat and her sister Suzette during Pat's teenage years, which, bizarre and uncomfortable as it was, filled a need. It was after one of their random weekend trips to town together, when Pat collapsed in a heap absolutely exhausted, that Suzette piped up, 'What's wrong with you? You're far too young to be so tired after just a few hours of shopping, come on what's up?'

'Nothing,' Pat replied. 'Just a bit tired.'

'Yes, but why are you so tired? Pregnant, pregnant are you?'

'No, I don't think so.'

'What you mean you don't think so? So there's a possibility then that you might be?'

'No, I haven't had sex for about four or five months now, not since Ray and I split up, there's been no one since.'

'Well, like I said,' went on Suzette, 'I find it a bit strange that you're so tired, maybe you should do a pregnancy test, just to satisfy my own curiosity.'

'No problem,' sighed Pat, anything for a quiet life.

Shock cannot begin to describe how Pat felt when the two blue lines appeared on the pregnancy test. Suzette started jumping around as if she'd won the lottery. But the words coming from her mouth showed her true feelings.

'Bitch! We knew you would be the one to come home pregnant, no baby father, no job, no money, you are hopeless, what are you? A complete waste of space, yeah, I wanna see how you're gonna tell Mum and Dad this one!'

Scans confirmed Pat's due date and how far along she was, her eyes wide open as she tried to digest that she was already six months pregnant. Her limited knowledge on pregnancy and childbirth raised questions in her mind; aren't you supposed to be sick when you're pregnant? Why haven't I been sick? What about missed periods? I had one last week…weight gain? Why aren't I getting fat? Pat dismissed these concerns, as she had no one to turn to and ask, and would never have dreamed of going to the doctor unnecessarily.

Reaching the 'blooming' stage of her pregnancy which followed shortly, when every woman feels at their best, skin glowing, hair shining, Pat looked and felt great. So much so, that Suzette, thinking her sister looked a bit too happy with herself, decided to put a stop to it. 'You know,' she said one day, 'when women are pregnant their skin gets messed up and their hair starts to break, it gets weak, it gets dull and before you know it, you look like an old piece of carpet.'

'Oh, I didn't know that,' replied Pat.

'Yes, well what do you know about being pregnant? I'm telling you, your hair and your skin goes to pot, sooooo….! erm let's cut it off? Yeah cut off your hair Pat! Do it now before the baby is born, you don't want to look like an old dog when you go to hospital to have your baby.'

Being the pliant, adoring, immature and inexperienced woman Pat was, she listened to her wise older sister who of course would never put her wrong. Would she? Pat sat while Suzette chopped and snipped her beautiful, Afro bob length mane. With each snip of the scissors Pat shuddered, at first Suzette cut through her hair as if running a marathon with haste and no precision, but as she approached the finish line her pace slowed as she admired her handiwork, like she didn't want it to end.

Afterwards as Pat viewed her new look in the mirror, picking up the dead chunks of her hair, fiddling and rolling them between her fingers she thought: My beautiful plaits, oh God what have I done? No, no, she tried to reassure herself, it was for the best and my hair will grow back healthier and stronger... Then, looking back at herself in the mirror she saw her sister's reflection. Suzette could contain her triumphant laughter no longer and rolled around the floor cackling hysterically and pointing. 'Look at you, you idiot! Don't you know a woman's hair is her beauty and a woman should never cut her hair whilst she's pregnant?'

Pat sat there looking at her own reflection in disbelief. How could she do that to me? She thought: I listened and trusted her, now look at me. Who did Pat see when she looked in the mirror now – a simple minded, gullible fool? Was this really her? Is this really me? It appeared so.

A month later, August 1986 and arriving two weeks early (No surprise, Pat was so stressed it's a wonder how he didn't arrive even sooner) Isaac was born. Pat's whole family were still disgusted, but when Mum came to see the two of them she sang from the rooftops.

'Oh Pat, you've had a baby to give to me, he looks nothing like you,' meaning that he wasn't dark in complexion, 'he could pass for my own son!' She was remembering her own son, Pat's little brother who never grew up, who passed away when he was just a tiny baby, the only child that had looked like her, and her side of the family. Isaac's fair complexion, bright blue eyes and jet-black straight shoulder length hair, reminded her of him. 'Yes,' she continued, 'he could be a Dubois, he looks just like grandpa Cyril, nothing like his father Ray, who was darker in colour than her or like you. 'She then added. 'I don't think he resembles his father's side of family at all.' A Dubois for real!

This was Ray's first-born too, and he decided to try again with Pat. Once again they proved to be incompatible, and it wasn't to be. So what now lay ahead for Pat and Isaac?

One of Pat's favourite films at the time had been the American hit 'Fame'. Of course, it was a dance movie, and all about following your dreams. Pat's life ambition now was to go to the States, and teach dance there. Having Isaac needn't stop her. Like the dancing itself, no one paid any attention or took her plans seriously, so she stood alone. She worked hard and saved hard. As the time for departure drew nearer, less and less was said about it in her family, but this was the norm. In her heart she wanted so desperately for them to acknowledge her goals and aspirations, she wanted desperately for them to share in her excitement about embarking on a new adventure, but her mind knew better: stop being silly you know that's never going to happen.

At the airport, on Tuesday 11th February 1987, Mum and Dad, Suzette, Karman, Marianne, Barbara and Claire came to see Isaac and Pat off. She had a bad, sinking feeling; there was no excitement, no happy words of wisdom, just silence from all her sisters. She felt as if they couldn't wait to see the back of her. She went to the toilets and cried her heart out and at one stage said to herself: I'm not going! But then she had to decide, which was the worst of the two evils; staying there with them or going into the unknown? So, rapid was the decision made, Pat quickly got on the plane with her son.

Pat enjoyed her stay in the USA. She was driven and focused, never, ever getting too involved in the family politics over there, although her instinctive nature was swaying her more and more towards them, the spirit of Grandma Nana Mar Christina kept her at bay. Then bad luck struck when Isaac became ill with acute pneumonia, and after two weeks in hospital they had to return home.

Pat's mother was pleased to see them both. In fact everyone was pleased, and all quick to remark, 'Well we knew you would come home, we knew you wouldn't make it. You're not woman enough to face life on your own without us.' Pat just smiled and tried hard not to take them on. That night as she chewed over the events of the day, she couldn't help but agree with what they had been saying. She was a failure, they were right! Perhaps they'd always been right.

She confined herself to the bedroom over the next few days using Isaac as her excuse not to mingle, trying to gather her thoughts and decide what she was going to do next. It didn't take long before a serious dose of depression took hold of her, she started to think that the world might well be a better place without her, and that Mum and Dad and everyone else could probably give Isaac a better life then she could ever give him.

Mum quickly picked up on this and asked Pat if she would rather return to the USA, quickly Pat said yes and straight away started making plans. As the time to fly out again grew closer, worries and concerns, particularly about Isaac became paramount. Pat thought: What would I do if he became ill again? Where will we live? Will I get my job back? What will I do if I don't? Mum then suggested that she would look after Isaac for Pat, so while she was away she would only have to fend for herself, which would mean a great burden lifted off her shoulders. Never once did she stop to think that there might be repercussions from her doing this.

With a clear conscience and peace of mind that Isaac would be cared for by her parents, going back to America seemed a much easier prospect for Pat. She arrived in the Big Apple for the second time, and in a very positive frame of mind, applying for a position at the New York Academy of Performing Arts, yes the Fame school no less. But what Pat really wanted to be doing was getting out there and fulfilling her passion – she wanted to dance, she had to dance.

She soon met kindred spirits, fired like her with the same enthusiasm for this exciting, pulsating, life affirming art form. Together they formed their own troupe, starting at ground level, street dancing for the New York citizens while one of their members busked outside the subway station. It was a beginning, and it was exciting. Next they love at first sight put together an inter-state tour of the east coast, from Boston all the way down to the Florida Keys, working nightclubs and music joints, wherever they could get a slot to perform.

Some of the venues were to say the least; dives, where the male clientele made it plain they wanted some extra moves from the girls. Though not exactly sheltered Pat was shocked by this sleazier side of the American way of life, as slick lounge lizards offered her drinks and occasionally a 'little something to make you feel good.' She could have been tempted, but always her ebony lady – part guardian angel, part conscience kept her prudent and safe while on the road. All the time remembering the God fearing morals and high standards her mother had instilled in her; she would skin me alive, thought Pat, if I ever brought more shame on the family.

Pat returned home from America after the best part of six months just one week short of Isaac's 1st birthday. The day was celebrated in Sheerness at Mum and Dad's place surrounded by her so-called family and friends. Pat noticed something disturbing had happened in her absence; Isaac was now calling her 'Pat' and his grandmother 'Mum' He wouldn't come to Pat when she beckoned him, and a distance was forming between them already. All Pat could think was that the sooner she could get him away from them and alone with her, the better!

As soon as possible she got a job, and quickly rented a flat for Isaac and herself, much to the disappointment and irritation of her mum, who had clearly been expecting her daughter to stay with her, or at least leave Isaac as he was. But moving to her own place was the best thing that Pat could have done for her sanity. It wasn't that her mum, her dad or any of the family was doing the child any harm it was simply that Pat didn't want her mother to instil the same somewhat skewed family values into

Isaac as had been her experience. Being independent wasn't easy. For the very first time Pat was actually a single parent in the true sense of the word – no partner, no extended family, no one. She had to do it all on her own, there was no one to call, or call on, no one to rely on. Many nights she would cry herself to sleep thinking: how will I cope? I can't do this parenting thing all by myself.

She would then look at Isaac asleep in his cot and see a light at the end of this very cold, dark, and lonely tunnel and somehow her heart would fill with joy, and through this joy she would find strength, peace of mind and the will to succeed. From then on Isaac became her strength, her focal point; as long as she had him she knew, she could face another day. And if she just painted that beautiful smile on her face, everything would be okay.

While Isaac and wanting a happy life for him was the inspiration behind that smile now, Pat had other reasons to be positive. She had worked hard in America, and since her return, and by careful management of her money had succeeded in saving up a small nest egg. She was proud of this achievement, something she had done alone, through her own ability and determination. She would be careful of that nest egg, as she was over her little boy, and somehow find a way to put it to work for him.

Chapter Three

Location, Location

There was a knock at the door. 'Are you expecting anyone,' Pat asked the au pair. Yes she could afford an au pair now. 'No.'

Pat opened the door cautiously. She didn't get many uninvited visitors. Her two elder brothers, Roger and Ronald were stood outside. Surprised and pleased, yet at the same time nervous Pat invited them in and, having been brought up in the traditional West Indian custom of hospitality, set about making them something to eat.

They talked for some time, about nothing much in particular, Pat smiling politely all the while and constantly offering more tea and coffee, trying to hide her uneasiness about what might lie behind this unexpected visit. She thought she must be in her brothers' good books for them to be so nice as to call round and see her like this. At the back of her mind though she kept wondering: have I done something wrong, and is all this pleasant talk just setting me up for a fall from a very great height?

It was Ronald who popped the question. 'How much do you pay for rent on this place?'

Without hesitation Pat replied, '£300 per month.' Then, in a small voice she asked, 'Why?'

'Do you know,' continued Ronald, 'that you could be paying a mortgage for that amount?'

Pat looked at him, not knowing what she was supposed to say to this.

Roger looked up from his newspaper and chipped in, 'Yes, you could. Ronald and I have been thinking about your situation – paying out all this money on a property that will never be yours, when you could be paying the same amount on a mortgage for a place that could be yours one day.'

Ronald sounded so sincere and knowledgeable, and when they had left she pondered on what he and Roger had said, toying with the idea of becoming a homeowner. Just imagine me, she thought, owning my own home at the tender age of twenty. The prospect began to really excite her, and the fact that her brothers wanted to help her achieve this was wonderful.

Buying a property would cost more money at first though, for a deposit and other expenses, she realised that. But she had a good job in the financial services industry in central London, commuting there every day from Gravesend. She could easily get a second job in the evening if need be. And there was already the money she had saved from her trip to America, her and Isaac's nest egg; that could go towards a deposit. She started to work out her finances and itemise what she would need. Some furniture and fittings she might have to buy new, others she could perhaps take with her or get second-hand. It all seemed quite possible.

Pat said nothing to anyone about her plan, just worked every hour that God could send and saved every penny. As the months passed and her account began to look rosy she decided that now was the right time to start looking at properties and to tell Mum and Dad what she and her two brothers had discussed. Unbeknown to her however Roger and Ronald had already told Mum, whose response to Pat's announcement was, 'You took your time to come and tell me!' Pat now felt so ashamed that she had kept this a secret, and knew she shouldn't have. Deep down, Pat had perhaps known that her brothers would have told Mum anyway.

Pat signed up with a series of estate agents and viewed

numerous properties within her price range, but none of them suited her. It was one Thursday evening sitting at Mum's that she got a call from 'Hooper Homes' about a house that had just come on the market. The agents said they had access to the property and wanted her to go and view it. Eagerly Pat asked Mum if she would like to accompany her. The place just wasn't right though. Returning to the estate agent's office afterwards Pat felt deflated and disappointed.

Longing to find somewhere, Pat began looking at properties just above her price range, and sure enough one came up: 22, Trevale Road, Rochester. She showed Mum the details. 'Lovely,' she agreed. 'But it's too expensive!' Undeterred, Pat persuaded her mother to go with her and have a look. By the time they arrived at the address it was getting dark, and the electricity was off in the house, but walking in Pat felt a real sense of calm, hope and joy. She turned to Mum. 'This is the one – this is it!'she exclaimed. 'This is the house I want!' Her mother laughed. 'But Pat, you can't afford this one!' Pat replied, 'Oh I don't care I'll find a way to afford it.' That night she couldn't sleep, thinking of all moneymaking schemes she could legally work at to buy the house. Then she thought: assuming I can afford the repayments, solicitor fees, stamp duty and whatever else, how will I get the mortgage in the first place?

She told Roger of her concerns. He said, 'It's not a problem, I'll sign on the dotted line for you.'

'What do you mean?' Pat asked.

'Well, all you need is another income to show on the mortgage application – so you can use mine!'

Well that was it for Pat. She shouted at the top her voice, 'Yes, yes, yes!' deafening Roger.

'Calm down, calm down,' he smiled.

'I can't believe it,' said Pat. She was over the moon.

'Well now the hard work begins,' said Roger. 'You'll have to save £1500 to cover your legal costs. I'm only signing on the dotted line for you, but it's your house, your legal fees, nothing to do with me! Ok?'

It certainly was. It suited her just fine. A house of her own! Pat smiled and thought: this is fantastic, everything is sorted; her brothers really were helping her. This was how their mother had raised them all; they were a family and here to support one another. Listen to your brothers, Mum would always say – they'll never put you wrong.

Each month Pat would buy things for her new house, till the dining room, every available space in her bedroom, and even the hallway of her tiny little rented flat were bursting at the seams with all her lovely new goodies. She couldn't wait for the big day when the removal van came to take Isaac and her to their new home.

Meanwhile it was time to finalise the actual purchase of the house and make everything legally binding. An appointment was made at the solicitor's office, and Pat, Mum, Roger and Ronald went along. It was just as Pat was poised with her elegant new Shaffer pen in hand, about to add her signature to the documents, when her solicitor said something that made her stop. He pointed out that once she had signed, she and her brother would each own fifty per cent of 22 Trevale Road.

Surprised, not to say alarmed at this, Pat turned to her brother and murmured quietly in his ear. 'This isn't what we wanted,' she said, 'the house is supposed to be mine. You tell him.'

'What's the problem?' enquired Mum.

Pat looked to Roger to reply, but he didn't. The solicitor then asked, 'Is there a problem Miss O'Neal?'

In a very timid, shaky voice Pat began to explain that Roger was only signing on the dotted line to help her obtain the mortgage, so the house was actually going to be hers, not theirs. The solicitor then explained if that were the case a separate document needed to be drafted and signed by both parties explaining this.

Pat said, 'Fine, OK, how quickly can this be done?'

'What's the rush?' said Mum.

'No, no rush,' replied Pat quietly. 'But I think the sooner we get this done, the sooner I can move in.'

(I do believe that my solicitor was a very clever man, and could read through the lines here). He smiled. 'You'll have a document to sign by the end of this week.'

'Thank you,' said Pat.

They left the solicitor's office, all somewhat upset. But Pat could see her Mum's brain was working overtime. She put her arm round Pat, who braced herself, knowing that whatever was about to come out of her mother's mouth she was not going to like. Here it comes she thought, that softly spoken voice that lays down the law. 'I think,' said Mum, 'that you should share the house fifty/fifty with your brother.'

The words echoed around Pat's head. This was supposed to be mine, she thought – my time, my independence, my house. Finally she gathered the courage to answer. 'No mum.' There, she'd said it.

Mother stopped in her tracks, gave her a stern look and said, 'Listen,' in her Dominican accent; boy now Pat knew she was angry. 'Listen I'm not asking you I'm telling you, you will share the house fifty/fifty with your brother. This is not open to discussion, and I won't tell you again OK? OK!'

A long burst of Patois, Mum's native tongue, now rang out loud and animated between her and her sons, a conversation that Pat was not privy to, for, as her mother well knew she did not speak or understand. Mum and Roger appeared excited about something though, while on the journey back to Mum's house Pat felt nothing but numb, withdrawn and once more pushed aside. Pat felt she had no choice but to accept owning half of the house.

The day the letter from her solicitor arrived was one to remember, for all the wrong reasons. Once again they all met at the solicitor's office. Taking a very deep breath and putting her best foot forward Pat stood tall and brave as the contracts were signed. Then, when it was time to make the down payment, Pat turned to Roger and asked for a cheque for his fifty percent of the legal fees and deposit. Roger started to laugh. Unable to see what was funny Pat repeated her request. This time he didn't laugh but gave the widest, cheesiest grin imaginable. 'Where do you expect me to get solicitor's fees and deposit money from?' he said.

There was an uneasy silence. Everyone looked at Pat then at Mum, then back at Pat. Finally Roger said, 'I tell you what, you pay the fees and the deposit and I'll pay you back.'

Pat thought about it for a while then said, 'I don't think this is fair. First you say you're just signing on the dotted line for me to get a house of my own, then you agree with Mum that you should own fifty per cent of the house, and now you want me to pay all the fees?' She wanted to say more, but the solicitor gestured to be silent.

'My advice to you all is to go away and think about this situation. Decisions need to be made, and my office is not the place to make them,' he said sternly. Then he turned directly to Roger. 'Mr O'Neal if you are to be a fifty percent share owner of this property, by rights you should pay fifty percent of the costs.'

Ignoring the advice of the solicitor Roger turned to me once more. 'Pat, pay the damn bill and let's get this thing over with.' With palms sweating and her heart pounding with anger and frustration, Pat picked up her chequebook.

But as she began to put pen to paper, her solicitor, once again reading between the lines stopped her. 'This is not the place to make hasty decisions,' he said. Mum then rose abruptly from her seat and vacated his office, with Roger and Ronald following reluctantly, leaving Pat behind, feeling lost, bewildered and totally deflated.

This time the journey back to Mum's house was quite the opposite; no patois was spoken, no excited, upbeat conversation. Pat felt the same numbness at being once more isolated, shoved aside. Her brothers were not silent though; far from it, their voices were raised and their tempers flaring. Never before had Pat seen them so angry. They seemed convinced that they had it right, and being 'fair' was irrelevant. Pat sat quietly in the back of the car, trying frantically not to allow her emotions to take hold of her. She closed her eyes, rested her head back, and tried to comfort herself. For a while it worked, or at least she managed to block out the harsh voices, the sound of the traffic, the music that was playing in the background. It was as if time stood still. Was she dreaming all this? She wanted to open her eyes again but dared not face the reality; that the dream of her home, her independence was slipping away, gone, crushed forever.

When the car came to a halt she felt so scared, and held her breath for a moment. 'Pat!' yelled her mother. Startled, her body tensed. She thought: What now – what else could her mother possibly have to say to her? She waited to hear more of the same anger, cussing and accusations of how ungrateful she was, that her brother was doing such a wonderful thing for her, and the only thing she should do was show him some appreciation, let him have half the property, but no she didn't want to do that.

What a selfish, self-centred, little no good-for-nothing bitch she was....

She couldn't believe it when she realised what her mother was actually saying...'You're right love, it's not fair, but nothing in life is fair, but what I will do is give your brother his fifty percent of the costs for purchasing the house OK love?' Was this was supposed to make her feel better, Pat wondered, make her jump for joy and think that all was fine now? She shook her head in disbelief and exhaustion.

So Mum lent Roger the money, and not once but twice -what he did with the first lot was anybody's guess. Eventually contracts were exchanged and the purchase was complete, the house was theirs, Pat's and Ronald's. It was agreed they would pay the mortgage one month each at a time, starting with Pat. And that was where it finished too; like tomorrow, 'next month' never seemed to come for Roger, who always had some excuse as to why he didn't have the money.

It was a struggle to find the mortgage money alone and some months her payments were late. Eventually Roger warned her, 'Well here it is, you live here with your child - I don't. If you want to continue living here, I suggest you make sure the payments are met on time.' Pat couldn't believe it, she was once again shaken, stunned, she didn't want to believe it, what was this really about? First her brothers come and disturb her life, which was standard, nothing special, but it was OK, she was surviving, and they plant the idea of being a property owner in her head. Then they say they'll sign on the dotted line to help her purchase the home of her dreams, only to leave her to pay the mortgage and the bills – a single parent. And this was supposed to be her family. Pat had to dig deep in her heart to find comfort and forgiveness now in order to welcome her brothers with open arms. Returning from work she would find their dirty overalls on the floor in the kitchen by the washing machine, her bathroom used and left in a state, her weekly shopping eaten and no food for her son or herself. Who could she complain to? Mum wouldn't believe her she wouldn't even listen. So what should she do? Paint her beautiful smile on her face and get on with it, because life wasn't fair!

When they turned up at her home at 3 o'clock in the morning telling her they were hungry, and to fix them something to eat, her mind was willing but her heart was heavy and hurting, she felt used and abused. She had no one to talk to about this situation; she was alone and had no choice but to bear the humiliation and distress of having the two of them constantly in her face, exploiting her compliant nature. Having to say nothing was the hardest part of it all, but she painted on her beautiful smile again and did as she was told, hoping that one day her silence, dutifulness and obedience would be recognised and she would be adorned with love and God's blessings.

It was then that Pat got reacquainted with Brad. Brad was the type of man that Pat thought she might marry, the type you would be proud to bring home to meet your parents – you know the type! So introducing Brad to Mum and Dad and the family as a friend was a breeze. Pat often wondered whether if she had said he was her boyfriend she would have got the same reaction.

Their friendship went back to the days when Pat had first left home, Brad having been a good friend of the boyfriend of one of her housemates. A Christian man with strong morals and beliefs, she felt very comfortable and safe around him, even asking him to play the role of her husband when she moved in to Trevale Road for the sake of the neighbours, which of course was no big deal, and which he was delighted to do.

Playing the happy couple, the perfect housewife and loving

husband came naturally to both of them, and this worked for a good while. Brad enlightened Pat, showing her the gentler side to life, and giving her a glimpse of what it was like to be treated with love, respect and care. He opened her mind to the true values of married life. He demonstrated that marriage was a two-way street; it was what you made it, and as long as a couple were both going in basically the same direction together, they would arrive at their destination in perfect harmony. This kind of considerate, sharing attitude in a relationship was a unique and liberating experience for Pat, until her brother Roger upset the apple cart.

It was a bright Sunday morning, and Pat and Brad were planning the day's adventures – a picnic perhaps, exploring the South Downs, should they take the bikes? That was Brad's thing! He loved quad bikes, mountain bikes, or plain old simple bikes. Or perhaps they would really do the happy couple thing and walk hand in hand across the yellow sea of dandelions, daisies and other wild flowers that seemed to bloom endlessly at this time of year in the fields.

Pat and Brad were sat in the peace and quiet of Trevale Road mulling over these pleasant possibilities when suddenly the front door flew off its hinges, and her dream of a perfect day fell to the floor alongside it. To her horror in the doorway, posed like the young Bruce Lee in his brilliant white karate uniform (gee) his black belt with its three gold stripes, a dominating presence, stood a young man. His assertive stance clearly reflected his attitude: he meant business. Pat didn't know whether to laugh, cry, jump, shout or scream. It was her brother Roger, his eyes looking through her, his gaze fixed on Brad. Fuelled with the fictitious notion he had been fed by various members of the family, and believing that Pat was unable to control any type of relationship, Roger felt that he was acting in her best interest, and of course at the same time looking after his own as regards the property. Pat had no time to think, as the questions came fast and furious, same as the punches that followed swiftly after.

That was the last time Pat saw Brad for many years, till she received an invitation to his wedding. What, she thought is wrong with me – am I really that damaged, that hopeless and irresponsible that they feel they have to interfere in my life at every opportunity. Pat had lost a good friend in Brad, one of the first people in many years that she could rely on. He had made her smile, made her laugh, and asked nothing in return.

Pat continued to struggle hard to keep up the repayments on the mortgage, working two jobs, looking after a young child it wasn't easy. Perhaps there was a way to split the bills? She decided to put an advert in a local shop window for a lodger. The response came one cold winter evening. There stood a young girl homeless and pregnant. Pat gave her the room, and helped make it as cosy as possible for the arrival of her baby. Neither one of them had much money, but they worked together as a team and got things done.

Then Pat made a mistake, one of many. She told Mum about her new lodger. It was stupid of her to think she would be pleased that not only was the arrangement helping with the mortgage payments and bills, but also that she was helping someone who was in need. Given the close bond Mother had with Roger, it was inevitable she would pass on this information to her son; that the room in the house in Trevale Road he had earmarked for himself, Pat had now rented out. He was not best pleased at the news and decided to pay Pat a visit. She knew he was coming and tried desperately to prepare herself. But no amount of preparation, organisation or conversation could prepare for the devastation that was about to be unleashed. Suited and booted this time, he arrived at the house and stated his claim in the most commanding, authoritarian manner. 'This is my house! And you out!' pointing to my young pregnant lodger. Pat said 'No! She is not leaving. I had to rent the room to help me pay for the mortgage. We have had his property for how many months now? Nearly a year in fact, and you have never contributed. I was struggling, I couldn't manage, so I had to do something, don't you understand that? So she is not leaving okay!'

His response was very calm and highly unnerving for Pat. She had seen what he was capable of and was waiting, stiffening her body in anticipation of the impact.

But he just repeated, 'This is my house and I want her out. I give her four hours, I don't care where she goes or how she goes, if need be I will put her out myself. Four hours.' Pat and her lodger cried and cried, till they felt that they were both about to enter a state of unconsciousness. Phone calls were made and boxes and bags were packed! Four hours to the minute Roger returned and escorted the girl out of the house.

Despondent and exhausted with the same old routine of going to work at 7 o'clock in the morning, her ideal home was always left clean and tidy just the way she liked it, everything in its place, polished waxed or watered, this was Pat. Wafting through the elegantly flowing interior, with designs, colour co-ordinations and ideas stolen from glossy home magazines would often be a cocktail of smells – greasy overalls and the fragrance of full English fry-ups enjoyed by her brothers. 'Not again,' Pat mumbled to herself one evening, picking up the soiled clothes left in the middle of the floor for the umpteenth time and loading the washing machine. It was beyond a joke. It had never been a joke. If Ronald didn't pay anything towards the house what right did he have to use it? He should not even have a key to the place.

Just then the phone rang. It was Mum. Should I tell her, Pat thought. Dare I tell her, about my feelings of despair, the way I feel my brothers are taking advantage of me? Her mind was racing: Do I tell her that they eat my food and leave my son and me hungry until the next pay day? Do I tell her that I feel uneasy leaving my home not knowing what state it will be in when I return? No, she sighed, I guess not. Mum had been talking a while as Pat weighed these options. Now Mum said, 'When last have you seen or heard from your brothers?'

Plodding on, carrying this burden back and forth to work each day, Pat finally gave in and told her mum, crying and hysterical, trying to explain to her that she had had enough, she couldn't cope with it anymore. Mum made it quite clear she didn't believe what Pat had to say, and didn't want to hear another word. Pat, deep down, had feared and knew this would be the reaction, but nevertheless had to make it known that her brothers were taking the piss out of her. After the conversation with her mum Pat felt so distressed that she changed the locks on both the front door and back door. Immediately after the locksmith left, Pat asked herself why she had done it. She was fully aware that this course of action could possibly cause World War Three.

A few days later Pat was hurrying to collect Isaac from the child-minder with only minutes to spare, walking as fast as her legs could carry her, planning some quality mother and son time at home with her Isaac. Little did she know Roger had other plans in mind. Arriving at the house and opening the door she was once again greeted by the unwelcome smell of work clothes and greasy food, sending shivers down her spine. Walking through the open plan layout she looked cautiously around the floor, expecting to stumble on a pair of overalls at any moment. Instead she saw her brother Roger, sitting at the kitchen table looking smug. 'How did you get in here?' Pat asked sheepishly. There was no verbal response, but Roger's his head tilted lazily towards the back door. It was battered and hanging to one side.

Instead of shouting and screaming – for she knew this was yet another battle she was not going to win – Pat quietly prepared some food for her son and made herself a hot chocolate, then led her son out of the room without a glance back, headed for her bedroom, and locked the door. There she retired for the rest of the evening. Eventually she heard the front door slam, and accepted the fact that this was the type of life she had no choice but to lead. It's not fair, but life's not fair. The old, empty echo went round and round her tired head.

Life in Rochester was a bittersweet experience. Pat had lovely neighbours and made a few friends, and came to terms with her brothers' antics. A year or so after the purchase of Trevale Road, her two brothers turned up one afternoon. 'Roger would like for us to get a loan to upgrade the property,' announced Ronald. 'Such as, put in new double-glazing, perhaps a new kitchen and to generally do some refurbishment.'

Pat foolishly became excited, as she hadn't been able to decorate for well over a year now. Roger carefully spelled out to her how much he wanted them to take from the equity of the property, and penny for penny how it would be spent. Any remaining money, he laughed, his jovial side kicking in, since he was in a bad financial predicament, with Pat's good nature, she would allow him to retain. Allowing no time to consider the facts and implications or more importantly the repayments of the loan, Roger produced an application form, ready filled out and requiring only Pat's signature. She happily signed, not thinking of the consequences. Roger and Ronald smiled and promptly departed.

As Pat left her house for work a few weeks later she was greeted by the post-man, who placed a letter in her hand. It was from the finance company about the loan for the refurbishments. Excitedly she opened the letter and found that the loan had been agreed. They wanted to know if there was a joint account, and if not whose account the money should be paid into. No longer was Pat excited, she was now anxious and concerned, turning this question over in her mind what do I do, what do I do? She and Roger didn't have a joint account, and if the money went to him, she doubted she would see any of it. If she asked for it to be paid to her, she would never hear the end of it. What on earth should she do? I know, thought Pat, I will call Mum. I think I know what she will say, but whatever the outcome she can deal with it.

Her mother wasn't home when Pat called, but she and Dad had a wonderful chat, just catching up really, on how Isaac was doing, and how things were with her. Pat asked him to tell Mum to call her when she returned home. Her dad asked if there was any other message. 'No message,' said Pat, though he guessed and could detect in her voice that something was up. He dropped a hint. 'I know things can't be easy with your brother in your hair constantly.'

With that Pat opened up to him and told him about the loan. Dad asked, was she crazy, had she lost her mind? 'Why?' Pat asked. Dad took a deep breath, calmed himself and began to explain what she should now do. By the end of the conversation though, Pat felt as if a weight had been lifted from her shoulders. She couldn't help but feel like a prat. Roll on tomorrow she thought while on her way to work the next day, knowing she was going to be late. I have two extremely important phone calls to make, and I believe they could change my life.

The following morning at 9am sharp Pat called her solicitor. 'Please can you draft a contract, stating that on receipt of payment of the full loan just approved, her brother Ronald would sign over his half of the property at Trevale Road to me.' This simply meant he would take the loan money, and she would have the house. I will then repay the loan, thought Pat, and Ronald will have the money to spend as and when he likes.

Pat couldn't wait for the letter from the loan company to drop through the door, and with it the cheque. As soon as it arrived she called Ronald, and of course he was down in a flash. 'Can't stop long,' he said. 'I'm in a hurry tonight get me the cheque and I will be on my way.'

'Um, not so fast,' Pat said quietly.

'What do you mean, not so fast? What, what do you mean? I've got to get going.'

Pat took the letter from her bag and proceeded to open it nervously and placed it in front of Roger. 'You need to read this before I can give you the cheque.'

'What bullshit is this?' exclaimed Roger angrily. 'I don't have time for none of this!'

'Well if you want the cheque you have to make time and read this.'

His face became distorted with anger, his eyes opened wide, as if he was mutating from Roger to Rex, T Rex, and Pat had become his prey. Trying to maintain a cool and poised demeanour she stuttered, 'S-s-sign… the contract and the money is…all yours.'

At that point Pat stepped slowly backwards. Her brother's eyes were full of disbelief, hostility and rage. Pat opened her mouth to speak, but she was full of fear, no words would come out. A second later her mouth was filled with his fists. Strangely enough she didn't feel the impact when her back hit the side of the kitchen work top, which broke in half, or the bombardment of punches that followed swiftly afterwards, she didn't even recall him leaving. She could only remember crawling on her hands and knees to the front door, to the phone, to call her mum and dad.

She heard her mother's voice: 'Serve you bloody right, do you think you can fight or blackmail your own brother?' Her father's response was totally different; he was horrified, revolted to think that her brother would lay his hand on her, for anything, let alone for money.

Pat took some comfort and relief that her father had been shocked and concerned for her safety. He at least was on her side, he understood. But it was the last straw. She realised that, in her case at least, being a homeowner was far from plain sailing. She stopped paying the mortgage, stopped paying the rates and all the utility bills, kept the loan cheque, and waited for the building society to repossess the house. Then she would move out. It was not an easy decision to make, nor an easy thing to do. Despite all that had happened Pat loved the house, and had thought of it as her home forever. Abandoning it in the manner she did brought more heartache and distress than she could have ever imagined. At times she thought, Pat you stupid cow! You could have just put up and shut up! But could she, and should she? She had looked in the mirror and seen Pat the successful homeowner, a woman of property, someone who could hold their head up high, someone to admire. But not for the first time, the mirror had lied.

The solitude she experienced in the weeks leading up to her departure was not entirely unwelcome. She attempted to fill the emptiness, the silence with activities and noise, packing and unpacking, music blaring. However when the music went off and she sat down, in the silence and the peace she could hear herself think, was able to become still and allow her feelings about herself and her family to surface until she became aware of her fears, as well as her strengths. She learned now that she possessed faith, and learned how to trust the power of solitude.

These weeks of solitude brought Pat much-needed clarity. She became clear about what she specifically wanted in her life, and what she did not want. She remembered all the things her family had done to her, the ways in which they had hurt her physically and mentally, the way they hurt her feelings, affected her emotions, she recalled the things they had said and the lies they had told her, and told about her. She remembered how she had trusted them to love her, care for her and protect her. She remembered how they had not done any of these things. Pat decided now she could no longer trust them and did not want to be a part of them, or be anything like them.

So, weigh up your options, choose carefully and make your decisions. Never let it stray too far from your mind, that whatever actions you take, there will always be a reaction.

Chapter Four

The Lodger

After spending so much time wallowing in self-pity at the disappointments she had experienced -her trips to America cut short, the breakdown of her relationship with Isaac's father and the loss of Trevale Road, Pat decided it was time to put her life back on track. A better job was the first priority; she scoured the newspapers, attended the job centre like it was her new school, but without result.

Then one day, overhearing a conversation about someone being offered a job, by tweaking her CV to suit – even though she was later found out – got her thinking. Sure enough, shortly after sending out a 'revised' CV Pat landed herself a very lucrative position in the financial industry, arranging mortgages and life insurance. Through her new contacts she rented a luxury, executive house in a very prestigious area, despite knowing that even on her high salary she couldn't really afford the monthly payments without working every hour that God would send.

With a small child it would be doubly difficult, but nevertheless Pat went for it. She had a point to prove. Her plan was to advertise for a professional person to rent the spare room of the house and help with the outgoings. She also saw this as a means to help integrate her and her son into the local community; as a young, black, single mum living in a predominantly white community, she was determined to fit in. Her lodger would therefore have to meet certain criteria; ideally be a young white professional male, like children, and to keep up appearances, be assumed by neighbours to be part of the family unit.

Months passed and no one responded to Pat's advert. Meanwhile the bills started to mount up, and as her desperation crept up she began to realise anyone would do, she just needed the room rented. Then, while on her way to work one morning she was offered a lift by the lady that ran the sandwich round on the business estate. I'm sure she eats all the sandwiches, Pat smiled to herself – does she really make any money? And her topic of conversation as usual was sex, sex and more sex, same thing different day. Pat didn't really understand why this subject was at the tip of this dear lady's tongue every time she stopped and gave her a lift – was she like this with everyone? And she was a married woman!

After several attempts at trying to get a word in, Pat allowed the sandwich lady to waffle on then casually, through this riveting sex chit chat, or monologue more like, Pat mentioned she had a room to rent. There was silence in the car for what seemed like ages till the sandwich lady then whispered something. Pat wasn't aware that she knew how to do that, always so loud, so brash and confident. The whispered remark was: 'I have the perfect lodger for you!'

Pat replied, 'Oh really – who?'

'My brother,' she replied.

'Your brother?' said Pat, somewhat taken aback.

'Yes, he's sleeping on my sofa at the moment. He's a good hardworking man, he has a good job – he's clean and tidy and very quiet. You won't even know he's there.'

Pat agreed to meet the brother and talk things over. Mark fitted her criteria perfectly; he worked, drove a lovely car, and was clean and tidy just as his sister said, and most importantly, he was white. Shame I don't find him fancy-able thought Pat!

Things worked out very well with Mark. He started doing jobs around the house and really taking an interest in Isaac, taking him on day trips, buying him toys and clothes, and asking Pat about his birth and early years. At first, Pat thought nothing of this, but after overhearing a conversation between Mark and one of his work colleagues about herself, she became slightly concerned. She said nothing to Mark, but sat back, thinking she had probably misinterpreted what she had heard.

Then Pat's mum called one evening, asking her how things were between her and Mark. She found this very strange having always told her mother that Mark was a very nice guy but not for her! She told her this again, and her mum asked 'Why, he works doesn't he?'

'Yes!

'He pays his rent on time doesn't he?'

'Yes!'

'He takes interest in your child doesn't he?'

'Yes!'

'So what's the problem?'

Pat explained: 'Mum, he's my lodger. I don't see him in any other light than that. He's really not my type!'

'So why do you think he keeps asking you about your pregnancy and the birth of Isaac? Now Pat I know you're not stupid, surely you can tell that he really likes you!'

Pat replied, 'No! Don't be silly.'

But Mum wouldn't let it go. 'Then why do you think he's asking you all these questions?'

After the disbelief, Pat felt a shocked, dawning, realisation that it could be true, that her lodger Mark was attracted to her… no, no, surely not! She shrugged her shoulders, shook her head and started to laugh to herself as she began to look back on his behaviour – yes, it was all starting to make sense now. Then suddenly she thought: Oh no, I'll have to ask him to leave – but what about the rent? Pat tried to make some sense of it. OK, he liked her – maybe, against her initial thoughts she liked him too – or could come to like him. After all she had said it to herself: he is a good man. As she turned this over in her mind, reality would then kick in and she would shake her head in dismay that the idea would even enter her thoughts. enter her thoughts.

After weeks of trying to keep out of Mark's way and not really having much in the way of conversation Pat decided that his continuing to be her lodger wasn't going to work out – neither for him nor her! So she asked him to leave. Mark asked if they could talk about it. She replied there was nothing to talk about.

'I feel rather embarrassed about the whole situation Mark,' she said. 'I had no idea I had given you any signals to make you think there is, or ever could be anything between us.

'Please don't worry!' exclaimed Mark. 'There's nothing to worry about. Would you like a cup of tea?' Pat shook her head, made a dismissive gesture with her hand and retired to her bedroom for the rest of the evening.

Things remained normal in the house for the next few months. Pat had begun to feel that Mark's crush on her had passed, when one Friday she received a phone call from her mum, to say she had collected Isaac from the child minders and was going to have him for the weekend. Pat thought nothing of it, as this was a usual occurrence.

Pat returned home from work, and everything looked as it should, except that when she put her key in the front door, it did not open. She tried again and still it would not budge. Flustered and agitated now, she saw that Mark's car was in the drive, so why was her key not working? Her imagination began to run riot – was he OK? Had something happened to him in the house? Had he got a woman in there – perhaps in her bed?

She tried the key one more time then picked up a brick. As she was about to smash the window, the door opened. Pat's eyes opened wide in amazement, her heart missed a beat: stood in the doorway of her home was a tall, handsome, white man dressed in a tuxedo and white gloves. In the most softly spoken voice he asked, 'Are you Miss Patricia O'Neal?'

Stuttering Pat replied, 'Y…Y…Yes.' Then sharply but quietly adding, 'and who the hell are you, and what are you doing in my house?'

The young man said, 'Please come in Miss O'Neil.' She proceeded into the hallway of her house, and there was greeted by the sight of dozens and dozens of red roses, shimmering in the light of a huge array of candles. Apprehensive and at the same time curious, she continued into the dining room. Stood there, tense with anticipation beside an exquisitely laid dinner table, was Mark. In a hushed voice Pat asked 'What's this all about?' was all she could think to say.

In an extremely nervous voice Mark replied, 'Please Pat, take a seat, enjoy your meal and we will talk afterwards.' He pulled out a chair and ushered her to it, placing his finger over his lips. 'Shush, shush …enjoy your meal.'

Like the obedient child Pat had always been, she ate the meal and waited. After the second full glass of champagne Mark arose from his seat, and in the most sheepish, uncomfortable manner she had ever seen, dropped onto one knee and proposed marriage. Pat sat in complete shock, speechless, as he continued his well-rehearsed speech, professing his undying love for Isaac and for her: how much he admired her, what a great mother she was, and how he felt he could be a wonderful father to Isaac.

'Stop, stop,' muttered Pat. Still he mumbled on. 'Stop!' she shouted. For the first time in her life she felt power, Mark bowed his head to the floor, she felt in control. Then from out of nowhere she just exploded in a long, loud roar of laughter. She looked at Mark's face which by now was red as a tomato with embarrassment, confusion fear and hurt.

'Marry you?' Pat said in a nasty, sarcastic tone. Where had that come from? Was there a touch of Suzette in her that she didn't know about till now, and which for the first time had reared its ugly head? 'Why, would I want to marry you?!' she went on bitterly. 'I don't think so! I don't love you, I don't even fancy you.' Just the thought, of him touching her, repulsed Pat. 'Ah, look, thank you for the lovely meal and all the effort you have put into this, but no, marry you? No – no way!'

There was an uneasy silence for a few moments. Looking at Mark's face, trying to read his mind, or what his reaction would be, Pat now felt scared.

As Mark rose to his feet, Pat, realising that perhaps her reaction had been somewhat over the top, and majorly unsympathetic, said in a very calm voice, 'I think it's best if you leave …I'm sorry.' Then as he walked towards the door she said kindly if slightly louder, 'I just don't see you in that way, I'm sorry.' He turned and looked at her, and without uttering a word gave a faint smile and went off to his room.

Immediately Pat called her parents. 'Mum, you will never believe what has just happened…'

But before she could finish her sentence her mother, sounding awfully excited and anxious interrupted her. 'Well, come on then, how did it go? Did you accept?'

Stunned, Pat shouted down the phone, 'Stop – wait a minute, you're telling me you knew about this?

Her mother went quiet.

'Mum! Did you know about this?'

'Yes, aren't you excited? You're getting married.'

'Oooh am I?' Pat retorted sharply.

'Yes, of course you are!' Mum's voice was typically domineering and patronizing. After about half an hour on the phone, listening to her mother praising Mark and saying how much he loved her and Isaac, and of course what a wonderful life they would all have, Pat went to bed with the day's unbelievable events weighing heavy on her mind.

The next day she woke up to the smell of freshly ground coffee and hot croissants with melted cheese wafting under her nose. Through one eye she saw a tray had been placed beside her bed. On it was a single white rose and a card that read simply: 'I'm sorry.' Pat then heard the front door close and the sound of Mark's car pulling away from the drive. Filled with mixed emotions she lay not really knowing what to do, or even think.

During the months that followed, marriage was never again mentioned; Mark remained her lodger carrying on as before, sharing the house as if nothing had ever happened.

It was almost one year later, in the summer of '89, that Mark, having been invited to a social gathering with his father, asked if Pat would accompany him. Without any thought at all, she accepted. She turned out to be the belle of the ball, the lady in red, a stunning black beauty amongst a room full of elite, white high society top rollers. To Pat's surprise everyone was so friendly, and made her feel very welcome.

Then, halfway through the evening, as she and Mark conversed with a couple, a question was asked, 'So when are you going to have the next one? Or are you going to get married first?'

Confused, Pat turned to Mark to answer for her. With a pleasing smile to cover the awkwardness written all over his own face he replied, 'Pat is a career woman, so I'll take the timing from her. Isaac is quite a handful at the moment, so we will wait a while.'

Pat looked at him very hard, but turned and smiled at the couple. The lady then said, 'Oh love, it's better to have them one after another so that the little devils can grow up together, and from what I hear from Mark, you had such a wonderful pregnancy and the birth was pretty straightforward, but I guess that's natural for your type.'

Pat thought: my type! She knew exactly what the lady was thinking. She replied, 'Well, you know, black people.'

'You're such a beautiful little thing, so clean, so tidy, why has Mark hidden you away all this time? And the baby – he must be getting big now, when are we going to meet him?'

Again Pat smiled. 'You'll have to ask Mark that.' Before she knew it she was playing along with the fantasy Mark had concocted about them for the rest of the evening.

Mark and Pat never discussed the occasion, and it was soon forgotten. He continued to be his usual charming, helpful self and from then on very quickly started to play a major role in both Isaac and Pat's life. It didn't take long before neighbours, friends and work colleagues were making remarks about them, 'What a wonderful couple they are! And what a good daddy he is – he takes his son to the child minder before work and collects him afterwards, and he's always out with his son, and what a happy child he is…'

Sitting in the lounge one cold, cloudy, miserable Friday morning, looking out across the South Downs and listening to the rain belting down, Pat decided she was not going in to work that day. Thank god it's Friday, she thought. Oh but what would Mum think? She's never taken a day off in 45 years, with her strong work ethics, shame they didn't rub off on me, oh well the weekend starts now.

But for some unknown reason she felt down, low, maybe even depressed. She decided: today will be a day of self-indulgence, she would sit and eat chocolates and drink sparkling wine all day, slopping around in her PJs and watching all the daytime soaps on TV. Since it was Friday, Mark would collect Isaac and take him to her parents, so it was OK, no need to worry about Isaac he was well taken care of.

So, Pat indulged herself that day – and indulged a little more, and then totally overindulged. By the time Mark returned home she was completely and utterly intoxicated, pissed as a coot. Mark tried to sober her up and put her to bed, but having a gut full of Dutch courage, and listening to his jokey innuendos knowing he could take advantage of her in this state, encouraged her to think: I know he wants me, so hey, what the hell, go for it.

It had been quite a while since she had indulged in a night of passion. Her inhibitions lowered by several pleasant hours of drinking, erotic fantasies and desires had begun playing out in her mind. Mark wanted her so much, craved and drooled over her and she knew it. The thought of offering herself to him at last, excited her now, and seeing him look at her in that familiar, longing way, she felt a sexual thrill at the thought of letting him kiss her, undress her, see and touch her breasts, her legs, her thighs and beyond…Then he could take her, mount and enter her, yes, yes, he could f*** her. This ultimate prize and pleasure she would give to him.

Pat stretched out her legs, lifted her arms and laid back on the couch in a seductive, sex kittenish pose. Mark's tongue nearly hit the floor with the invitation. He did not need any more prompting. In his masterful way – the same capable, all commanding and efficient way he had organised the candlelit dinner that night, he rose supremely to his task. Mark took control, his lovemaking technique confident, comprehensive and energetic. He was clearly very aroused as he thrust rhythmically away.

For Pat, however, the initial excitement at the thought of finally surrendering herself to Mark fizzled out, as soon the mechanics of the act began. That was the problem really, or part of it – the mechanical, robotic way he went about it all. Pat couldn't accuse him of lack of enthusiasm it was just that neither her body nor her soul now shared his enthusiasm. Her giving in to him, she realised sadly, had been the result simply of boredom and frustration, at the end, when Mark climaxed so triumphantly, she was still bored and frustrated, as well as regretful now. Why oh why had she weakened? What had been the point? She had never felt any attraction to Mark on a physical or any other level, and for all the passion she had experienced during the sex act with him, she might as well have been doing the washing up. Come to think of it a sink full of dishes would have been a lot steamier.

The next morning Pat woke with a pounding headache, and Mark in her bed. She lay there stiff, unable to move, unable to talk. A soft voice asked, 'How are you feeling? Are you OK?' She couldn't answer; perhaps it was the shock, the realisation of what she had done. 'Would you like some coffee?' Slowly she nodded her head. 'Yes please.' Mark said he now planned to spend the day at home with Pat, stating yet again that he wanted to look after her. She however insisted he go out and spend the day playing football or fishing as he would normally on a Saturday. She really needed some time to herself.

When he had left the house, Pat called her mum and told her she had spent the night with Mark and had sex with him. Giggling with excitement her mum said, 'There, I knew things would work out. He's a good man.' She then launched into talking about wedding plans, gabbling on for a good half an hour. Pat thought: I only said I had sex with him, not that I loved him! She then heard her mum shout, 'Pat? Pat, are you listening to me? Now come on, pull yourself together, you've done the hard part, you've slept with him, from here on its plain sailing. So I'll see you and Mark on Sunday for dinner and we'll run through some ideas I have for the wedding....'

Pat must have smoked a hundred cigarettes that Saturday, trying to come to terms with what she had done, and how it was going to affect the rest of her life; marriage to Mark – the thought alone sent shivers down her spine.

Mark returned home in the evening armed with Pat's favourite Chinese take-away, a very expensive bottle of pink bubbly, and wanting to talk. She listened half-heartedly to his extravagant plans for the wedding and what he wanted to do with his life and how many children he wanted – how many children? The phrase replayed over and over in Pat's mind – it meant sex with him, sex and more sex. No, she thought in horror, I won't do it.

However Pat acknowledged that there were things she had already done in her life, which were not in her own best interest. A lot of the time these actions had been a reaction to fear. She accepted that she had been an unconscious participant in the creation of pain and discomfort throughout her life. Recognising this fact, she now found herself asking: well why not, was he that bad? Did he not know how to do it? Or, more disturbingly, was her real problem that in fact he was really OK? Pat needed to find answers, and she felt the only way to know if this was right, was to let it, the sex that is, happen again. And so, during the following two weeks, it of course happened again and again and again.

It then became part of the punishment, the punishment Pat had handed out to herself, the punishment that she felt she deserved.

Why? I hear you asking? To backtrack, Pat's first sexual experience had been one that left her somewhat confused; although it was new and exciting and gave her to some degree the intimacy and closeness she yearned for. But the words 'the sex was great, but that's all that was great,' still played with her mind. So to her sex was not a pleasurable activity, it was a chore, the punishment that became part and parcel of what a man would expect in return for a good relationship. It was what she had to give up to Mark in return for his contribution towards the bills, the upkeep of the household, and of course the role he played as Isaac's father. This selfless act would wash away her sins, she believed, and one day she would become pure again.

Mark settled down with a gardening magazine, intent on spending yet another day at home with Pat; he just wanted to be near, he insisted, to look after her for the day if need be. That day, and on two more separate occasions, after each physical encounter with Mark, Pat felt sick. Why? Eventually she accepted the fact that he really did repulse her; the mass of hair covering his body like a werewolf, his stubby fingers, and his smell – not that he was dirty or unclean – he just made her feel physically sick! And when she started to be literally sick, she finally said No! No more, she just couldn't do this. From then on Pat kept out of Mark's way, she was out all the time, she put a lock on her bedroom door – she just didn't want to be part of this anymore.

She actually started feeling a lot better in herself, and that she had done something rather radical, barring her bedroom to the man she was supposed to be marrying. What would her mother think? She laughed to herself!

But the physical sickness became more frequent and constant. Although she hadn't had sex now for over three months, a passing comment from one of the girls at work got Pat thinking: no? She couldn't be – could she? In constant denial, yet with her mind also working overtime she bought a pregnancy test. To her despair there appeared the two blue lines. Without hesitation she reached for the phone book and proceeded to call every termination clinic listed. Finally she found a private practice that would take her in immediately to carry out the procedure.

Trying desperately to contain her fear and panic, and holding back the tears that were almost stifling her, she called her mum and asked if she would collect Isaac from nursery. Knowing nothing of her daughter's plans, she happily agreed. For the next three days Pat played a part, swanning around the house as if she hadn't a care in the world, while stealing moments to express in private the heavy burden she was carrying, crying herself to sleep the only source of temporary relief from her pain, guilt and fear.

Sitting on the train, hardly knowing where she was going or what to expect, Pat's phone rang. It was her mum, absolutely hysterical. 'What the hell do you think you are doing!?' she bellowed. Without giving Pat a chance to respond, she then switched to her calm, commanding tone. 'I suggest you get off the train at the next stop and be there to collect your son from nursery as I will not do it, nor will your father or Mark. We all know what you are up to, and we are totally against it, and disgusted that you would even consider it as an option.' Had Mark found the yellow pages she had left open and called Mum? Is that how she found out? 'You are about to marry a man that truly loves you, how the hell do you think he feels that one, you never told him you are pregnant, and two, you are about to abort his child' Without taking a breath, she continued, 'Like I said, I suggest you get off the train at the next stop and find yourself at home.' Pat had no choice but to miss her appointment at the clinic and go to collect Isaac.

That day her plans had been thwarted, but Pat didn't give up. She didn't want this baby, and she didn't want Mark in her life. She tried everything that she could over the next few weeks to get Isaac looked after, money in her pocket, and the precious time to go and do what she felt she had to do. Due to fate, circumstances or the hidden workings of God's will, the end that Pat felt desperate to pursue did not come about. In August 1990, Ilana was born. Pat found her the ugliest baby she had ever seen, a picture of her father no less. But she is my baby I thought, my baby girl and I love her dearly.

Mark and Pat stayed together, on her part for the sake of the children, though for how long she would be able to bear the situation she did not know. The couple moved out of Pat's luxurious rented mansion and bought their first home together, and were there for a further two years after Ilana's birth. During this time Pat grew strong, independent and focused. She had made friends in her local community and had great work colleagues, always on hand to help and support her and the children.

Pat's faith in the Lord was at its peak, knowing that with God's grace he would change her false beliefs and give her the strength to heal the wounds she had allowed to fester throughout her life. Still the demons she now had to face were those of her family. And she knew that healing these injuries would take tremendous strength, patience and faith, which could only come from the Almighty God. But the question remained: who now stared back when she looked in the mirror? That face, was it Mark's partner – really? Yes? No? If not, then who was it…?'

* * * * * *

Here as Trisha, I say to you: if you're going to gain something, gain respect and confidence. And if you're going to hate something, hate the false idea that you are not capable of fulfilling your dreams.

Chapter Five

A Night of Fear

There was more to come with Mark. It was the autumn of '89, and, under duress, Pat was being led from jewellers to jewellers in the search for the ideal engagement ring. Ideal according to Mark, that is.

'This one will do."

'No it has to be perfect,' exclaimed Mark. 'I'm tired, I've had enough, this one will do, its fine.'

But Mark insisted otherwise, still they marched on, and on to the next shop, and the next. 'This one looks like my mum's…'

'Fine, great, lovely, get it then, now can we go? Come on, let's go.'

As they left the shop the heavens had opened, creating a fine mist of invisibility. Heading to the car in a hurry Mark stumbled over the bags of shopping that lay on the ground at the bus stop. A poor lady, more water than clothes, stood there soaked from head to foot.

'How far are you going love?' Pat asked her. 'The buses don't run very often around here?'

The look of gratitude on her face said it all. She was in the right place at the right time and had met the right person and it was as if all her birthdays and Christmas had come at once. She had stood there at this desolate bus stop for over an hour, hungry, cold, and tired, freezing from ice-cold drops of rain. She looked at Pat as if she was an angel sent to rescue her from the harsh elements of Rochester High Street.

They all got in the car. As the lady gave each precise direction, Mark accepted them with a sigh; a huff, a puff; this journey would take far longer than the usual twenty-minute drive up the road. His expectations of an afternoon of heavy petting, stroking and fondling, leading into an evening, a night of blissful romance, was ebbing away. For Pat, as well their passenger, the detour was heaven sent. She had escaped.

They arrived at her house. 'Please, won't you come in for a coffee?'

'No thank you, it's okay.'

'How about a cup of tea?'

'No, really it's okay.'

'It's not every day you meet someone so kind and generous, the least I can do is make you both a hot cup of tea, or do you smoke, maybe you can come in and have a cigarette with me, I just want to show my appreciation.'

Her home was small but neat and tidy, clean and comfortable. Pat couldn't help but notice the short sharp intense glares Mark aimed in her direction. She smiled to cover the awkwardness.

'Don't I know you?' asked the hostess. 'Your face looks so familiar.'

'I don't think so.' Pat looked closer and examined every line and crease on her face. She was absolutely hopeless with names, but brilliant with remembering faces, and this was not one she had encountered before.

The lady sighed. 'I don't know, there's just something about you that looks so familiar.'After a momentary quiet pause she then exclaimed, 'I've got it! Now I know – do you have a sister called Suzette?'

Pat hastily murmured something like 'no.'

The lady continued. 'She has a sister called Karman, who lives in Chatham.'

Once again Pat replied, 'No'.

'I'm sure that was it – you look so much like them, well more like Suzette actually.'

At that point Pat had no choice but to come clean. 'Yes I do have a sister called Suzette, and yes Karmen is my sister too.'

'Oh. Well, I do understand why you would deny them. I know you guys don't talk any more. It's a shame, 'cause what happened, it happened so long ago, maybe if you made the effort, things would be all right now. I know Karmen and I'm sure she has forgiven you for what you did.'

Hearing this last sentence Pat remained calm. 'And what exactly, did I do?' she asked.

'Look, I know and you know what you did, but it's okay if you don't want to talk about it, that's fine too, but I do think you should try and make up with your sister – that would be the right thing to do.'

Me make up with my sister? The words swirled round in Pat's bewildered head. Again she asked, 'What did I do?'

'Well you know it wasn't exactly you, it was Isaac.'

'Isaac?' Pat replied with a slight panic in her voice now. 'What did Isaac do?'

'Now you're playing games, there is no need to get on the defensive, I know and understand that he's your son and like all of us mothers, we will go to the ends of the earth to protect our children, like I said it's been awhile now and maybe a good time to make up with your sister.'

By this time, Pat's head had started seriously swinging. She had no idea what the hell this lady was talking about. What had Isaac done? What had she done? What had someone told this lady, that she felt she needed to apologise and make up with Karman for? Pat made herself comfortable in her seat and insisted her hostess spill the beans, tell her, explain to her what she was talking about. As the story unfolded Pat was beside herself. Pat and Mark left and headed straight to Mum's still shaken, angry and frustrated.

Pat blurted out nearly in one breath all that the lady had told her. Mum's response was nothing out of the ordinary; same old, same old, 'I don't believe you' attitude. The most she said was, 'Who is she? Who is this lady?' She was getting nowhere fast with Mum.

Pat and Mark drove directly to Karman's house. There was no answer, so she shouted again, knocked harder and louder, bang-bang-bang, but still no response. Pat sat back in the car, made herself comfortable and turned to Mark. 'We're not going anywhere,' she insisted. 'We're staying right here till she gets back, she has to come home sooner or later and I'll be waiting.' The fire raging beneath Pat's skin was uncontrollable. For all the years that her family had taunted her, called her names, abused her, taken liberties with her, she could digest and inhale all of it, but talk about her innocent child? That was a whole other ball game! Hours passed and Karmen still hadn't returned, and Mark's patience was starting to run out. 'Okay we'll come back tomorrow.' They waited for at least another two hours, still she did not return. They went to Mum's, asked her, as she knew the movements of every member of the family, 'Do you know where Karman is?' She refused to answer. 'Oh, I see that's fine, just fine.'

They were sluggishly going back to the car, with the hope that Mum would recognise Pat was so very upset and distraught over the whole situation, and perhaps offer some words of kindness to settle her aching heart. But no, it was Dad who called her aside and whispered quietly, 'I don't understand why your sister would say such a thing, why your other sister just stand by and listen, without saying a word, without putting her straight, without correcting the wrong that she was doing. Like you I am hurt and ashamed. You don't use innocent children as a pawn in adult s***. Anyway your mother called her the minute you left here yesterday and warned her you are on your way round, angry as hell. I, believe she has gone round to Suzette's, if you want her that is where you'll find her, I'm not telling you to go there and cause any trouble, well I know you're not that type. But that's where she is.'

Pat didn't waste a moment. Breaking the motorway speed limits they were off to Gravesend. They were greeted by some kind of spur of the moment party going on. Marianne was down from Milton Keynes and of course Karman was there, with her son. Pleasantries were exchanged and she and Mark were invited in. They drank and laughed, soaked up the atmosphere, all the time waiting for the right moment.

'Anyone for a snack,' announced Suzette. 'I fancy some spicy chicken wings, how about you guys?'

'I'll help,' said Pat, and followed Suzette out to the kitchen.

'What's up with you?' snapped Suzette when they were alone. 'Do you think that you can fool me? Don't you think I can't see through that so-called beautiful smile that you paint on your ugly face? So what's up?' Sharp as ever, no putting anything past her!

Pat told her. But before she could even get to the part that went: How could you sit there and listen to this crap?

How could you let Karman talk so much nonsense, so many lies? Suzette turned and said, 'If I was you, I would knock her out, I would make her pay, use my innocent child to gain friends? Hell no, no way, I'd let her have it.

Go on, she's here, right here right now – show her what you're made of, show her the woman that you claim to be, go on, box her down.'

Pat didn't see the conversation for what it really was: manipulation. Suzette had fuelled the fire that was burning within her to a temperature that could no longer be contained. 'You!' declared Pat, pointing accusingly at Karman. 'You wicked evil person, you! How could you?' 'What are you talking about Pat?' asked Karman.

'You know exactly what I'm talking about, and if you don't, let me explain can you tell me why you would tell people that Isaac was the cause of Edmund's death?!!!!'

'I don't know what you're talking about. I have never said that to anyone.'

'Then why would a complete stranger tell me this fantastic, pathetic sad story – the one you told her about Isaac and Edmund?'

'I'm not listening to this.'

'Yes you will, even if I have to tie you down and sit on you, you will listen to every detail, every disturbing fact, every stomach churning lie. Now where should I start? Oh yeah, apparently we were at Mum's, having some kind of argument, the lady couldn't remember what it was about exactly, but we were arguing, shouting, screaming, you know how it goes, you got vexed, argument ends with me telling you to get out of my mother's house, you run off upstairs to the bedroom, meanwhile, Isaac had overheard the confrontation and took it upon himself to mimic the conversation between him and Edmund, that in itself would be a great act, taking things further Isaac supposedly opened the front door and ushered Edmund out. Edmund being only a toddler, yeah right, ran out into the road and straight under a car.

So my darling sister, explain yourself – because my recollection of Edmund, is that he was born and died after nine days, so if I'm not mistaken, I am now 23 years old and my son is three years old. So can you explain how the hell Isaac could be blamed for his death? By the way, I had Isaac when I was 20 years old and Edmund was buried on my 16th birthday. You do the maths.'

You would think that if anyone had the right to be angry, it would have been Pat, if anyone were to let loose a couple of slaps it would have been Pat. But no, Karman was faster. She stepped up in Pat's face. Well this time Pat was not going to be a doormat to anyone, so she fought back. Not quite fought perhaps, but all those years of doing martial arts with Roger and Ronald paid off. Suzette sat back with glee in her eyes – egging her on to punch Karman, kick her. Pat, blinded by her emotions, let rip.

Karman got a good hiding. It was only when her son came downstairs, after hearing all the commotion, shouting, screaming, banging and clattering, horror filling his eyes when he saw Pat standing over his mother about to put the boot in, that he screamed out 'No auntie, no!'

Embarrassed now Pat stepped back, allowing her nephew to come between her and Karman. She thought maybe he shouted some abuse but it didn't register. He helped his mother to her feet and she turned to Pat and said, 'You will pay for what you've just done.'

The rest of the evening at Suzette's was spent in quite a sombre mood. Pat only just noticed that Mark had left. Very little was said about the dramatic events. There was a knock on the door. 'Who is that at this time of night?' Suzette mumbled to herself as she walked into the hallway. Marianne and Pat sat and waited with baited breath, as in behind Suzette came an unfamiliar figure. The first thing Pat saw was the blade, a machete, a massive machete, yellow marigold gloves, a balaclava; he must have had hundreds of layers of clothes, on for his hooded coat was standing out at right angles like the Michelin man. This was no joke, Marianne started screaming, 'Oh my God, oh my god, what is this, what are you doing?'

The man calmly replied, 'Which one of you is Pat?' There was a deadly silence. I couldn't believe it. I was shocked, numb – speechless. For all that my child and I had been through it appeared that my life was going to come to an end at the hands of my sister. I couldn't answer couldn't say a word. Again, his anger more intense he repeated, 'Which one of you bitches is Pat?' To Pat's utter amazement, Suzette stepped forward. 'I am Pat' she said. With that he lifted his arm above his head, Pat screamed and Marianne said, 'No, no I am Pat.' Pat then said quietly, 'Hey guys, it's okay'– with a deep breath 'I am Pat.'

He told us to 'stop f****** around' and that it made no difference to him: 'all you bitches can get what I've come here to give to her.' He stood there brandishing the machete, swinging it above his head then he stopped, walked over to Pat and put the blade against her neck. 'Are you fucking Pat?' She didn't answer, couldn't answer even if she had wanted to, it was impossible. He turned to Marianne and did the same, the blade pressing against her neck, 'Are you Pat?' Like Pat she couldn't answer.

Karman then walked quietly and confidently into the room. 'Now,' she said with a grin on her face, 'not so cocky now are you?' Everything seemed to go in slow motion, everything was hazy and muddled, and nothing made any sense. Yes Pat was angry, yes she was mad, and upset, yes she had confronted her sister about her lies, yes she had slapped her, and yes they had had an altercation; but did this give Karman the right to send a masked man with a machete to Suzette's house to kill her – to kill all of us? She must have lost her mind – she must be crazy.

The man waited patiently for a nod of the head, a sign to carry out what he had been paid to do. Praise God Pat's prayers were answered. He couldn't do it or wouldn't do it, either way he left. Karman left too, grinning, smiling and laughing out loud, 'Bitch! Teach you not to fuck with me!'

Pat didn't really know what to make of this whole situation or how to handle the fall out. Marianne's way was to cry and get hysterical, Suzette's was to cuss Pat, she told her straight up, 'This was your fault, if you hadn't had a go at Karman none of this would have happened.'

Then suddenly there was another knock at the door.

Petrified the girls all sat and looked at one another. Who was brave enough to go to the door? Pat said, 'I will go this time, I'll go, this is my mess.'

'No don't be stupid this is my house,' piped up Suzette. 'I'll go' Marianne's hysterical cries made Pat's blood run cold. Bang-bang-bang went the door again. Was there any way they could check and see who it was before they opened the door? Yes, yes there was. Pat ran upstairs and looked out of the top bedroom window and down at the front door. She was surprised to see it was the police.

She shouted down to Suzette, who cautiously opened the door.

'Good evening,' said one of the three officers stood outside.

'How can I help you officer?'

'Hmm, just checking all is well this evening.'

'Yes, shouldn't it be?'

'Okay madam, can you confirm who is in the house presently?'

Suzette ran through the list of names asking the officer what was this was about.

He continued, 'So, I would be correct in saying that everyone is present and accounted for and all is well.'

'Yes, what is this about?' Suzette asked firmly.

'Well, I'm really sorry to have to inform you that, a phone call was received from the Metropolitan police at our local police station here in Gravesend, warning us that there was going to be a bloodbath at this address tonight. Well as you have assured me that all is well, we will station a patrol car outside the house for the next hour or so then patrols will be carried out at 30-minute intervals. But if anything was to occur in the meantime please do not hesitate to call 999 OK?'

The girls sat in absolute silence for ages. All Pat could think was that Karman had gone mad, crazy, finally lost her mind. For all that her family had put her through, never would it enter her own head to do something like this, so what was to be done now? Suzette got on the phone to her ex-husband Ivan, who came down with his brother then she called Roger and Ronald who also came. Marianne called Steven and he turned up. Pat had no one to call. All the children were huddled together in one room at the top of the house, in the loft conversion and given a strict command not to come out of the room unless Aunty Suzette, Aunty Marianne, or Pat came to get them, despite what they might hear. No matter the screaming, shouting and crying, they were not to come out of the room. Every inch of the house was now defended, protected by the sisters' own personal soldiers, tooled up and ready for action.

No one else came to the house that night but in the morning they went in search of Karman. First stop, her house she wasn't there just the boyfriend. First they asked him nicely where she was, then again, third time still no answer he had it coming; he got the beating of a lifetime, that was meant for Karman. Meanwhile she seemed to have disappeared off the face of the earth.

About five months later she turned up again. Nothing was ever said about that terrible night of fear. She was never to apologise for the lies or the masked man incident, never a word was said. As for Mark, well what can Pat say? They were all scared out of their wits, words couldn't really describe their feelings, but to get in his car and drive off, leaving behind never mind Pat, the woman, he wants to marry, but the child that he claims he loves so much? Need one say any more? Maybe, his departure, and being an unwilling witness to the brawl between Karman and Pat was an insight into what was to come.

Mirror, mirror on the wall, who am I? Pat sighed as she gazed at her reflection yet again and asked herself the question that had eluded her all her life. In the last few months she had been lied about and misrepresented as a person. But who was the real person, the real her. Whoever it was seemed as hard to perceive as ever. Did they even exist?

> The ultimate measure of man is not where he stands in moments of comfort and convenience, but where he stands at times of challenge and controversy.
>
> Dr. Martin Luther King Jr.

> Throughout life people will make you mad, disrespect you and treat you bad. Let God deal with the things they do, 'cause hate in your heart will consume you too.
>
> Will Smith

Chapter Six

Christmas of Destruction

After Moses, Ronald's eldest son from his first marriage died things changed dramatically for Pat and the rest of the O'Neal tribe. Pat was struggling hard to come to terms with her prior vision of Moses' death. Again her beautiful ebony skinned black lady had appeared to her, showing her pictures of the coffin, all the children in their school uniform, her brother Ronald, and once again there had been images of strong black women. At the time she had known what she had to do, what she ought to do.

Now Pat's mind was preoccupied with the notion that if only she had been stronger and more robust, perhaps she would have taken the risk of telling her other brother Roger, or Moses' mum about her vision, and maybe, just maybe Moses would still be here today. Guilt overwhelmed her, and she did the only thing she knew how to do, turn to God for his guidance. You have to believe that the Almighty God has a plan for everyone; when God's plan is fulfilled only then can you move on to the next phase.

Mum and Dad finally decided to set a date to go back to Barbados to live. After hearing this for the last ten or fifteen years, none of the family really took it seriously.

But this time it seemed they meant it, and were packed and ready to leave by the 28th October 1991. Pat and her siblings all went to see them off at the air-port and in some dismay and disbelief hugged and kissed them in the departure lounge then watched wide-eyed as they disappeared through customs.

After the fond farewell no-one really knew what to do. Pat

and the others sat around the airport drinking brandy to drown their sorrows, till Roger rose slowly from his seat and said, 'Well that's it, Mum and Dad are gone now, it's down to us to keep the family unit together. Come on let's all go home, and we'll meet up at my house next weekend OK?'

Well, the next weekend never came. Christmas came and went, Pat, Isaac and Ilana spending it by themselves in Kent with no other family member in sight. Pat missed and pined for her family greatly – for her parents, for her siblings; even at the age of twenty five and after all she had been through with them already one would think she would be happy to see the back of them, but no, she missed all of them like mad! With Ronald still grieving the loss of his son and not coping very well with the constant reminders of him in London, Pat invited him to come and stay in Kent with her and her children for a few weeks. Ronald accepted, and it turned out to be a wonderful time for Pat, the bond between her and her brother becoming very strong and meaningful to her. She had never really experienced a friendship with one of her siblings before, one in which she felt like an equal and was appreciated for just being her.

When after three months Ronald returned to London, Mark started to make his presence felt. Before it had been just the odd phone call, but now he was coming to the house and causing a nuisance. It got so bad that on many occasions Pat had to call the police to ask him to leave, though all they would say was that the house was his too, and they could not remove him from the garden if he was not threatening her or the safety of her children. So, night after night Pat would put the children to bed then see a figure appear in the garden, he jumped the fence and sat with his back against the wall, just staring into the house through the patio doors. This unnerved Pat and made her feel quite uneasy.

After several months of this silent harassment Pat couldn't take any more, and realised she might have to flee her home, but such a move would need careful planning and organisation.

Meanwhile another Christmas was by now fast approaching, and Pat had received an invite for her and the children to go and celebrate the festive season with her younger sister Marianne in Milton Keynes. She gladly accepted and decided that if in the New Year the nonsense with Mark hadn't stopped they would have to leave permanently to escape his pestering, that seemed to be taking over her life. So their bags were packed and they were on the way to spend a lovely time with Marianne and her daughter Sherri-May, before departing Pat asked her friend and neighbour Sandra to please keep an eye on the house for her, over the holidays as she would not be back till the New Year.

Christmas went off with a bang, lots of partying, drinking, eating, and fun and games. The children had a wonderful time. As the New Year came around Pat wanted to go home and put the central heating back on, collect the mail and make things nice for the children to return to. She called Sandra and told her, I'm planning to come down by train this weekend. For some reason however, too much partying and drinking probably, she didn't make the intended trip, so the following weekend she called Sandra and apologised for not seeing her as she had said, telling her not to worry, she'd be down the next week. Whilst on the phone, she harped on to Sandra about how wonderful Milton Keynes was, and how great she and her sister were getting on; if only she had the money or could sell her house quickly she would move there. Sandra lowered her voice and sighed. Be careful what you wish for, was her cautious response, the concern expressed not only through her words but her tone: Don't do anything in haste. Pat understood, and knew exactly where Sandra was coming from. As much as she might love her family now, how could she be sure they really loved her?

Another week passed and Pat still hadn't got to Kent, so she phoned Sandra to apologise yet again. But before she could even begin the conversation, Sandra jumped down her throat and started to rant and rave about how she had said Milton Keynes was so nice and how much she would love to move up there. Pat was shocked and when she managed to get a word in replied, 'Yes, and what's the problem?'

Sandra said angrily, 'If you knew you were going to move to wonderful Milton Keynes why didn't you just say that?'

A little perplexed, Pat said, 'I haven't moved, I just said I would like to.'

There was a very uneasy silence then Sandra said, 'Are you there?' Pat could hear a tension in Sandra's voice now; it had become shaky and low, almost like she was an undercover detective. 'Pat I want you to level with me,' she said. 'Tell me the truth – have you moved to Milton Keynes, as in, moved out of your house?'

Pat paused for a moment before replying with a nervous, half-hearted laugh, 'Sandra, what's going on?'

'I suggest you get on the next train and come down here,' replied Sandra. 'But when you arrive, come to my house first, do you understand?' Pat had never experienced Sandra's sergeant-major attitude before; in all the years she had known her, it was the first time she had been demanding. Pat thought: I guess she means business.

When she arrived at Sandra's they sat and drank brandy, for a while, but she couldn't help but feel that Sandra was stalling her, waiting for something. When her husband Gary returned home from work they all wandered over towards Pat's house. The short walk seemed to be taking forever, Sandra and her husband going at a snail's pace behind her, whispering, taking quick glances at her and bowing their heads. As for Pat, she felt as if she were in a race with herself. I need to get indoors, do what I need to do, she thought, and get back to the children in Milton Keynes.

Pat stepped through the front door of her house and found herself up to her knees in water. Squelch, squelch, she waded through the hallway, her mouth open wide, her eyes flickering from left to right, forward, centre, up and down around and around. Entering the dining room, then the lounge, she clapped her hands to her face and screamed: OH MY GOD!! She stood in complete shock: where her French patio doors had stood there was a gaping hole in the wall. Slowly she turned her head and surveyed the rest of the room, still numb with disbelief; large chunks of plaster were missing from the walls where wall lights had once been, water was dripping from the ceiling light fittings, and black paint had been thrown up the walls and on the carpets. Daubed across one wall in large letters of black paint were the words BITCH, GO BACK TO WHERE YOU CAME FROM!!

As the downstairs of her house was open-plan, Pat could see through to her kitchen, or rather where it had been; all that remained was a cupboard and a sink. She turned and walked up the stairs. Behind she heard sniffles from Sandra, but had no time to pay her any attention. She needed to see what else had been done to her home. The first room at the top of the stairs was her bedroom, and here they had had a field day too. Next was the bathroom, but what bathroom? The bastards had even taken her bath! In Isaac's room, the loft conversation there was black paint everywhere total destruction! Pat stood frozen to the spot she couldn't talk, or even think. She could hear Sandra crying, and now her fear turned to anger thinking: what the hell is she crying about, this isn't her house!

Sandra's husband Gary, though also looking downcast suggested calling the police. Sandra's sniffles and crying had now become hysterical. 'I'm sorry, 'I'm sorry,' she repeated, 'I'm sorry, oh my god I'm so sorry.'

Pat tried to console her and hug her and explain. 'It's not your fault. I know you didn't do this, or have anything to do with this. So what are you sorry for, why are you saying you're sorry?'

Sandra's crying reduced to a whimper, then, in an almost volcanic eruption she exploded, 'I was there! I was there, I'm sorry Pat, I saw them from my house, I thought it was you…'

'What do you mean you saw them – you saw who…?' The words tumbled out of Pat's mouth.

'Your sister, Karman, and Mark, the removal van, I thought you was moving, I didn't know what to think. You just told me how much you loved Milton Keynes.

What was I supposed to think?' With this Sandra broke down and cried again. Pat stood in a daze, she felt her head spinning, her whole world churning and mixed up, upside down, inside out.

Gary put his hand on Pat's shoulder and explained. He said when Sandra had seen the removal van she had called him at work, very upset. As she truly respected the friendship that she and Pat had developed, she couldn't believe Pat would move out without letting her and Gary know, and coming to say goodbye. But when she saw Pat's sister she assumed it was all above board.

Pat then butted in with a question. 'Why did you think I would be moving and not be there?'

'Well we did find that strange at first,' replied Gary. 'But we figured Milton Keynes is a long way from Kent, so perhaps you stayed that end with the children, while your sister came to this end to pack for you.'

There all three then stood for a moment in silence, till it

was broken by an unknown voice. 'Hello, what's going on here then?' Wading through the water- logged house appeared two burly police officers. One of them took a look around and found it highly amusing, while the other lent a more sympathetic ear. 'I can understand you may feel you're in no fit state to talk about what has occurred here, but unfortunately we need to take a statement.' Sandra and Pat together proceeded to tell the police officers what little they knew about what had occurred. One of the officers asked Pat if she knew of anyone she could call to come quickly and secure the property, meaning the hole in the wall. 'No,' she said quietly. He said not to worry, and made a phone call.

As Pat stood and watched the workman board up her house, the police officer handed her the crime report, which rendered her house uninhabitable. The officers departed with a list detailing her possessions that had gone missing. Sandra and her husband then left in a daze and returned to their home without saying a word to one another. Pat was left standing alone in the broken, unfamiliar place she once called home. What did she do now? Where did she go? She fell to her knees and cried uncontrollably. With all the things that life had thrown at her, she had always remembered the words: The Lord does not give you more than you can carry. But this time she didn't believe those words; the weight was far too great. Using Sandra's sofa as a bed for the night, Pat asked the Lord for strength and guidance. She had called Marianne to let her know what had happened, and why she wasn't returning to Milton Keynes just yet.

A couple of days later Pat received a phone call from the police. It was good news according to them; they had located some of her possessions, and would like her to meet them to identify the items. When the police gave the location to meet,

Pat gasped, 'No! You must have that wrong.' They repeated the address. Pat then asked what items there were. It was most of the things she had reported missing apparently. 'Are you able to attend?' they asked. 'Yes,' she replied, tears running down her face, 'I will be there shortly.'

Sandra's husband offered her a lift. When they pulled up outside her sister Karman's house her heart almost stopped beating. Nerves, passion and anger started to swell within her. The officer invited her in and asked if she recognised anything. She didn't have to look hard. Karmen was there. 'How can you do this to me?' Pat said to her. 'I'm your sister – Isaac and Ilana are your nephew and your niece. Thanks to you they have no home. My house is uninhabitable, why?' Pat couldn't take in much more, everything else that was said from that point forward was just a blur, and then she was back at Sandra's house.

She did recall at some point the police officers telling her she could press charges, and have Karman arrested for being in receipt of stolen goods. Even when it came to light that Mark had given her new fitted kitchen and bathroom suite to his sister, still she declined to take action. Subconsciously, although being told constantly by Sandra and other friends that she should, she should, she should make Karman pay for her involvement with Mark, for destroying her home, she couldn't do it. Instead she submitted an insurance claim, which would of course replace what she had lost, and she thought, cover the hurt. She thought if she could now just file the whole event away in her mind, she could put it down to a bad experience and forget what her sister had done.

Unbeknown to her at the time though, the desecration of her home was to be just the tip of the iceberg. It was to be just one thing after the other to destroy her. The next bombshell was Karman and Mark's announcement that they were now the happiest couple on the planet. What could Pat say other than, 'I wish you both the best of luck.'

Brother Ronald wasn't impressed though. 'Why didn't you slap her?' he remarked. 'If that were me, I would.'

'OK, OK,' Pat said. 'I know, that's just not me. She's pregnant again and she needs someone.'

Pat and her children stayed with her sister Marianne in Milton Keynes while the insurance claim was being processed. She also kept in tight contact with her brother Ronald, though not sure why; maybe because to her he was more of a father figure than Roger, or was is it that she was actually able to bring out the hidden, softer side that attracted women to him? Yes, she was his sister and loved him dearly as her brother, but if they were not related she felt she too would be attracted to the smooth, sweet talking, loving kind and generous, macho but sensitive mini Bruce Lee the Third.

On the other hand there was Marianne. One might have thought that Pat's sister would be accommodating and sensitive to her situation, but oh no, she had no thought or consideration regarding Pat's feelings and difficulties, from the diplomatic lies she had to constantly tell her children, the upsets, the upheaval, the changes of schools and the loss of their own simple possessions and friends. All this was insignificant to Marianne, who complained at the slightest thing the children did, or the noise they made, and threw cheap remarks at Pat; grateful as she was to have somewhere to stay, she was back to a life of being belittled and humiliated, and it didn't take long for the 'ugly' jokes to rear their ugly head once more.

Pat's mind was numb her heart was cold. For sure, if people don't ask how you feel, what you think, what you want or what you know, there is no way they can know who you are. When people don't know who you are they mistakenly believe they can do anything they want to you, and of course, they will. When this happens it's up to you to take a stand for yourself. But Pat was in no position to make a stand; she was empty, emotionless and fatigued.

Ronald came down for the weekend to Marianne's place, and witnessed the situation first hand. When he was leaving he called Pat aside. 'How the hell do you put up with this?'

'I don't have a choice,' said Pat. 'I have nowhere else to go.'

Sharply he replied, 'Marianne is not the only sibling that you have you know.'

In private moments, behind closed doors, Pat as always searched the face she saw in the mirror, looking closer and deeper, asking it to reveal its true self. But as always, like the Sphinx, the face remained silent.

* * * * * *

When someone finds themselves in a situation of sheer desperation it's difficult to see through the murky waters that surround them. Healing is the only way forward. Let us start by promising ourselves to be strong – let nothing disturb your peace of mind. Think only of the best way forward, forget about the mistakes of your past and give no time to criticise those who hurt you. Use the psychological feature of your being that is motivation, to take action towards your desired goal.

Chapter Seven

Violence, Abuse and Lies

Pat lay there still and stiff, the only things that moved were the tears running down her face. She did not wipe them away or try to stop them in any way, as she knew, this was a major part of the healing process that the Trisha, she was trying to become, needed to go through. People always say don't cry, don't cry, but crying is not a bad thing as long as you know what you're crying about and crying for. Trisha needed to heal, she needed to acknowledge hurt and pain, she needed to come to terms with all the bad memories the demons and all that made her scared and frustrated. In order to gain strength and to grab a hold of reality, face it and deal with it.

Pat's stomach started to regularly churn, upside down and inside out. Unable to take the situation at Marianne's anymore, she saved, begged and borrowed from everyone she knew to rent a temporary house for the children and herself. It was a dirty nasty, empty shell of a house, bare and lonely; although she tried with all her poor means to make it homely as possible, this place could never be home. But Pat truly believed that as long as she had sight of her children, they would get through this. The adjudication officers were dealing with their insurance claim, and day by day she prayed for the cheque to arrive in the post. It would be their salvation, their deliverance, the only way she could see it possible for them to ever return to their home.

Embarrassed by where they were living Pat constantly made excuse after excuse and gave pathetic reasons why family and friends could not come over to visit. She felt cut off from the world and at her wit's end. It was just at this point, at a time when she was most vulnerable, that Pat was caught off guard. She agreed to allow her sister Suzette to come over. Suzette turned up with her new boyfriend and Marianne in tow. Pat didn't have the strength or energy to dismiss them at the front door, so invited them in. Marianne walked around in silence but Pat could sense and see the disdain and condemnation on her face.

Suzette on the other hand had no qualms about voicing her disgust. 'Where is your table and chairs?' she sneered. 'Did Mum raise us eating dinner off newspaper on the floor? Don't you have a TV? What do the children do after school without a TV? Forgotten how to use a paint brush have you? Come on you can do better than this.'

Pat's eyes welled up with tears as she stood there shivering, trembling with nervous anxiety, while Suzette loudly criticised the little she had. In her mind she just wanted to shout and tell her: It's not my fault, I didn't burgle my own house, how the hell do you think I feel? I'm not accustomed to living like this. But instead she broke down, weeping and wailing, moaning, crying and crying some more. She felt faint, her head spinning, the lower half of her body weak as if her legs were going to give way beneath her. Then as her body swayed she suddenly felt cradled, and bathed in concern, as a tender voice whispered, 'Don't worry, you will get through this.' In her hand was placed a piece of paper and the same voice whispered, 'Call me.' Her wailing became a whimper as she struggled to pull herself together.

The arms that had cradled her belonged to Suzette's new boyfriend, Pat had never met this man before and didn't even know his name. But yet he had compassion and sympathy for the children and her, he was an angel that the Lord had sent to show Pat that she had the strength to get through this, and believe that there were still good people around. Whatever one's point of view, this man had been sent from God, for what he did next was shocking, scandalous and incredible. Pat was mesmerised as he turned now to Suzette. No longer speaking tenderly or whispering he said to her, 'It's over, please don't call me again. I am totally ashamed to have been a witness to your disgraceful, despicable behaviour towards your own sister. How on earth do you sleep at night?' With that he left. Suzette and Marianne went shortly after.

Less than a week passed before Suzette was on Pat's case, on the phone constantly badgering her to allow her to play the big sister role and to do the right thing by her children and her, by allowing her to have the kids stay. Each time she called Pat would fight with herself; wouldn't the children be better off staying with Suzette, just until the insurance claim came through and their house was ready for them to move back into? But how would she cope without them? Her children were her strength, they give her the will to survive, the strength to carry on. How would she get through each day without seeing their faces? Pat would end this battle by asking herself, am I being fair to them, fair to myself? Or fair at all? But life is not fair is it?

Eventually Pat gave in, and gave her sister her wish, and with it the opportunity to play her hero, her saviour, the big sister role she thought she had always wanted. Half-heartedly Pat packed her children's bags and took them down to her sister Suzette's house in Gravesend. In her heart she knew she was making the biggest mistake of her life, but at this late stage she simply didn't know how to get out of it. All she did know was that nothing good could possibly come out of the situation, but having no alternative she painted her beautiful smile on her face, pushed all the negative thoughts to the back of her mind, and tried desperately to see the visit as a positive move forward.

The practical arrangements proved fine. Pat would go to work during the week, and go down to Gravesend on Fridays to spend the weekend with her children. She and Suzette drank and partied during these weekends and even started raving regularly at the famous Hill Top Club. Then Suzette asked Pat for the child benefit to be paid directly to her. It was only fair, she claimed, as she was now looking after the children. Pat didn't see a problem with this, and only asked if she would mind waiting for a couple of weeks, just until her work pay cheque came through. But Suzette objected to this.

'But I'll have no money to travel to work or to eat,' Pat pointed out. 'I won't even be able to travel down to you at the weekend.'

Suzette's only response was, 'This is not my problem!'

Pat dared not argue, and reluctantly handed over her child benefit book.

Her children at least seemed happy enough, till one day Pat received an unexpected phone call at work from Suzette. 'Pat I think you should come down, like now,' she said bluntly.

'Why? Pat asked.

'Why? Get on the bloody next train, don't argue, don't question me just come down!'

'I'm at work, I can't just leave so do you want to tell me what's wrong?'

'I can't find Isaac; he's been missing for hours.'

Pat was shocked, both by the news, and by the tone of her sister's voice, so cold and emotionless, not seeming worried, concerned or anything of the sort. When she asked her what had happened Suzette merely repeated herself, and the phone call was ended.

Sheer panic was flooding Pat's mind; what had happened? Was her child OK? She had no money, how would she get there?

Quickly she explained to her boss that she needed to leave, there was a family emergency in Gravesend. Without hesitation he said: Pat, go, and even gave her the train fare.

When Pat arrived Suzette was calm, almost completely unfazed that Pat's child, her nephew was missing. I asked again what had happened. Suzette said that he had sworn at her, and she simply gave him a smack, after which he ran off, and that was the end of it. Instantly Pat did not believe her; she knew her child and swearing was not him.

'Where did he go?' Pat asked.

'I don't know,' Suzette shrugged.

Pat was already sick with worry, and had no time to argue. She had to find her son. She searched for hours, looking everywhere she could possibly imagine, parks, and shopping centres round the local neighbourhood. There was no sign of him anywhere. Hours passed and she was on her knees. Had he been hurt? Was he safe? She cried, her son was alone, upset, he needed his mummy and she needed him. She went back to Suzette's house and in the room that Isaac and Ilana shared, sat on her little boy's bed and sobbed. She had to pull herself together. Think Pat, think, she said to herself intently, where would you go? Maybe he had walked to his school, in hope of seeing a friend or a teacher. Pat calmed herself, till her sobs were replaced by a small glimmer of hope, telling herself yes, that was where he would be. At that point she heard a noise, a small sound. She turned to look around the room and there it was again. What was it? Controlling herself she listened carefully now, waiting for the sound to resume. Yes there it was again, a small, sniffling, whimpering sound.

'Isaac?' she said quietly. 'Isaac is that you? Where are you darling?' There was no reply. The room was practically empty, compared to the rest of this grand Edwardian property that

Suzette owned. It was bare, cold and minimal. Yes it had the essentials, the bare essentials a bed for her children to sleep on, a wardrobe containing their simple belongings and that was it. She looked under the bed, pulled back the covers, looked in the wardrobe, and even the drawers. 'Isaac? The little sobs came once more. She turned back to the wardrobe and pushed it a little, and to her horror there he was, in the tiniest gap, huddled up just crying.

She wanted to grab him and hold him, but he looked so vulnerable, so shaken she didn't want to scare him any more than he had been. The look in his eyes was unfamiliar, glassy and withdrawn. Pat spoke softly, she told him, 'Mummy is here.' Slowly coaxing him out of the tiny gap, he finally fell in to her arms, where she held him tightly, hugged and kissed him. Her child was there with her; he was safe. Pat couldn't begin to express her relief, but how worried she still felt for her son's safety. They sat in silence. Silence teaches you many things. It teaches you how to listen and how to hear. It teaches you how to feel and how to translate into words what you're feeling. When you can't translate what you're feeling, silence allows you to go deeper into yourself and find the peace that surpasses understanding, a peace that enables you to move forward even when you don't understand. Most of the time, silence is a good thing; but there are times and circumstances when silence will kill you. A killing silence can destroy your identity and your spirit. It can kill your heart and your soul.

'Isaac' Pat asked, 'what happened?'

Through his sobs he said, 'She beat me Mummy.'

'Who beat you?'

His voice trembling and his body shaking, my son had been terrorised. 'Aunty,' he said. 'She smacked and smacked and smacked me with the wooden spoon, she wouldn't stop.'

A smack, thought Pat, she said she had smacked him for swearing; a smack that was all, nothing more. She tried to ask why she had raised her hand to him, but he was so distressed, his eyes puffy and his face swollen. She gently examined his body only to find a multitude of weal-like marks and imprints of the wooden spoon. Pat saw she would not be able to get any more information out of him.

Pat walked down the stairs full of rage. She wanted to kill Suzette, but there was no way she was going to start screaming and shouting, or she could be the one that ended up dead. After the way Suzette has treated my son and showed no remorse, she thought, killing me would be a breeze. But my son is in pieces, that outcome is the last thing he needs right now.

Pat addressed Suzette in a small, but stern voice. 'I have found Isaac, he is upstairs, holding back the sniffles and the tears, he's safe.'

Suzette carried on with what she was doing, reading the local newspaper I think, showing no interest whatsoever. 'Suzette, what exactly happened in here today?'

'I told you already, he swore at me, he got smacked, that's all,' she said in an aggressive voice.

Pat stood her ground. 'No, no, you see I know my son, I know he wouldn't swear at you. Come on what really happened?'

'He swore, I told you.'

'No, I don't believe it, he wouldn't, I know him he's not that type of child, he doesn't swear, especially not to you.'

At that moment one of Pat's nephews, Marlo came down the stairs. The look on his face said it all; he looked pale, washed out, and in total distress. The eye contact was intense. He and Pat looked at each other and she knew he would speak the truth to her.

'Marlo?' she asked. 'Do you know what happened?'

Keeping eye contact with Pat, Marlo nodded then turned to his mother; he looked so frightened, traumatised even, yet his mouth opened and he started to explain to me, but now the eye contact was with his mother Suzette.

He said, 'Aunty, Isaac and Aiden were playing Scalectrics, and I think Isaac may have won the game, because I heard Aiden say 'Isaac you f****** cheat.' He slapped Isaac in the face, and Isaac just looked at him, so Aiden said it again, 'Isaac you're a f****** cheat!' Isaac said 'No I'm not a f****** cheat.' Aiden ran down the stairs to Mum and said that Isaac swore at him. And Mum took the wooden spoon from the drawer and started to beat him, and beat and beat him real bad, I tried to pull her off him, I thought she was going to kill him Aunty, she just wouldn't stop, and she was hurting him real bad.' As he spoke Marlo cried so much, it was if he was feeling the pain that his mum had just inflicted onto Isaac.

Pat turned to her sister, her heart pounding in her chest. Suzette's eyes said it all, she knew Pat was totally pissed off, and that was putting it mildly. Yet Pat couldn't even speak, so horrified and disgusted was she by her sister's behaviour and attitude towards Isaac, knowing how she treats Ilana like a little princess, she couldn't find words to even begin to explain how she was feeling. Talk about kicking someone when they're down, this was now primetime for Suzette, who proceeded to take total advantage of the situation. The belittling and 'ugly' jokes flooded back with a vengeance. She screamed at Pat. 'You're a useless mother – an ugly, useless mother! In fact, you're just useless, just ugly and your son is just like you. You're not a woman you're a child just like they are.' Pointing to her own two children, she pushed Pat against the wall with her face inches away from hers and said, 'Yeah, Miss Ugly, you heard me and what you gonna do about it?'

Just as Pat thought that was it, she'd said her piece, Suzette lashed out. The blows to Pat's face left the imprint of each of the rings that Suzette had on her fingers. Pat fell to the ground covering her face, only to receive kicks and punches to her stomach and back. Weak and wounded, Pat was unable even to entertain any notion of fighting back; instead she lay there and took the beating, waiting till Suzette was finally finished.

She then crept upstairs and painfully washed the blood from around her mouth and soothed the bruising round her eyes with a cold flannel. She then crawled slowly into bed with her children and settled them down for the night, desperately trying not to allow them to see her battered and bruised face, or hear her stifled moans and groans from the physical battering and the mental pain she held inside. She stayed with them that night and for the rest of the week, albeit out of Suzette's way.

During that week Pat thought about her options. She couldn't take her children back with her to Milton Keynes, since through not going into work she had lost her job and had no money left apart from £4.00 in her purse, along with her return train ticket. What on earth was she going to do?

Her sister Marianne came down to Suzette's that weekend, having heard what had happened, though her visit was not specifically to see Pat, she spent most weekends there anyway. Marianne and Suzette made a plan to rave at the Hill Top Club for the coming Friday night, and asked Pat to join them. Pat was hardly in that frame of mind, having no money or clothes, and quite frankly didn't want to go out, or be around the two of them. But Suzette was a very manipulative person, and one who did not take no for an answer. She pushed and pushed until Pat gave in, but she really was not in the mood for this.

So they dragged Pat up to London with them and went to their favourite hair salon, which of course was in the heart of Brixton

High Street. They were greeted by some familiar faces in the adjoining male barbershop, a clientele of six black, fine looking, handsome but don't get too close type men, a combination of: Denzil Washington in Dejavu (suited and booted), Tupac (guys from the hood) and Wesley Snipes (you know what I mean, in his black leather trousers, skin tight top and full length coat).

The ladies salon owner, a Miss Queen Latifah wannabe, came plodding over to the sisters, trying desperately to walk in her platform shoes, and dressed in multi-coloured skin tight leggings, a top about 4 sizes too small and with bright golden yellow weave in her hair. The outfit alone scared me, never mind her full-on loud, brash Jamaican accent, which filled the whole salon when she spoke. Suzette and Marianne explained what they wanted. Then the hairdresser looked at Pat. 'And you – wha' u want?'

'Umm oh no,' Pat said, 'I'm fine thank you.' Suzette stared and shouted at her, 'For God sake! Get your bloody hair done! Can't you see the state it's in?'

'No I'm fine,' Pat repeated. Suzette knew she didn't have the money.

'For fuck sake! Sit down Pat and get your bloody hair done!'

Pat wasn't going to argue, she was so drained. She sat down, and the hairdresser worked her magic, as some would say. When everyone was done and it was time to settle up Suzette and Marianne took their money from their purses and paid for theirs. The salon owner then turned to Pat '£15 please.' Pat just looked at her, and the lady repeated her request.

Pat turned to Suzette and said quietly, 'Which one of you is paying for my hair?'

Suzette piped up, 'I didn't say I was gonna pay for your hair.'

'No,' Pat replied in a small, mousy voice. 'But you told me to have my hair done and you know I don't have any money, so

I did, and now the lady needs to be paid.' Still whispering she then said, 'Marianne? Are you paying for me?'

'Me? No!'

Pat stood there not knowing what to do. Turning to Miss Queen Latifah she said quietly, to avoid embarrassment, 'I'm sorry, but I don't have any money.'

The lady stood back, placed her hands on her hips in fighting stance, ready for a confrontation. 'What!' she bellowed at the top of her voice. Silence then fell on the salon, all eyes on Pat. Leaning in slowly like a lion stalking its prey, the owner came up close and personal, in Pat's face and roared, 'Ya nah leave here till me get me money! Ya hear me?' Pat was so scared at that moment, she wanted the ground to open and swallow her up. She just couldn't bear the embarrassment and humiliation, her eyes swelled with tears. Then her sisters started laughing. 'We're just joking, you know, we're just playing around Pat.'As they paid the lady and left the salon, Suzette and Marianne continued to show just how funny, how highly amusing they found the situation. Walking from shop to shop while Pat trailed behind like the lost sheep, they laughed and giggled, offering Pat the odd glance to ease their conscience (if they had one). They swapped ideas on what to wear, Pat stood around like the outsider she was once more. Dare she complain, hell no!

Even though her sisters had bought her a new outfit, and paid for a new hairdo, Pat was still not in the mood to go out, especially with them; she just wanted to be with her children. The date of the planned rave arrived. Pat bathed her kids and put them to bed, and proceeded reluctantly to get ready for the night out. Once they got to the venue, she listened to the sweet reggae music, had a few brandies and began to relax and unwind a little. Pat noticed a man over the other side of the bar, they had a few moments of eye contact, and she thought to herself: 'What the f****** hell is he looking at? Can't he see he's wasting his time? I'm so not interested; I'm not in the mood! I just want to be alone and enjoy the music.' Then he began to make his way over; oh no, she thought, go away please. He asked her to dance.

She replied, 'No, I'm OK thanks.'

Looking into her eyes he said, 'Can I buy you a drink?'

'No,' Pat repeated.

'What's wrong?' he asked. 'Come on let me buy you a drink and maybe we'll have a chat.'

'No.'

'Well, would you like to dance?'

'NO.'

'What's wrong?'

'Nothing! I'm fine.'

'You have the most beautiful eyes, you may be smiling but your eyes are so sad. What's up?' There was a slight pause 'your eyes, I noticed them from across the bar, beautiful but sad.'

Pat's emotions ran high.

He asked again. 'Let me get you a drink.'

This time she nodded and said quietly, 'OK, yes please, a brandy.'

On his return he passed her the brandy and repeated his other question. 'Why do you look so sad?'

'I'm not sad, I don't know, nothing I guess.'

He went on and on. 'Maybe I can help, you just look so down.' At this point Pat burst into tears, he gave her his number and said, 'Call me, my name is Chris.' And with that he left.

The sisters came back from the ladies and before Pat could speak, Suzette asked, 'Who was that talking to you – what did he want?'

'Why are you holding a piece of paper?' Marianne asked.

Pat explained.

'Did you give him your number,' Suzette asked.

'What number?' Pat mumbled. 'I don't have a number, I don't have a mobile, I don't have a home phone, I don't even have a home and I daren't give him your number.'

'Are you going to call him? Suzette said.

'Hmm,' Pat sighed. 'No, I don't think so.' She ripped up the piece of paper she was holding and threw it away.

The end of the night came, and the three of them made their way to the car. Then Pat saw Chris. He had parked his car just a little way away from them. Suzette giggled and ran over to him. 'My sister forgot to give you something.'

'What's that?' he asked.

'This,' she said, and handed him a bit of paper with her home phone number on.

Chris smiled sweetly. Pat really wasn't fussed if she ever saw him again, her mind was focused on her children, not what next man would walk into her life; after the ones she had already had, she really wasn't interested.

The next morning, Saturday, Suzette banged on and on to Pat about whether Chris would call her. Pat didn't know if she was genuinely interested and wanted her to be happy or, was she just taking the piss! Or perhaps she was just looking for another issue to use against her. Deep down Pat knew. But later that afternoon, the phone rang and it was Chris. He and Pat spoke for a little while. He seemed polite enough, and generally interested in Pat, he wanted to take her out, he said 'Nothing serious, let's just go out for a nice meal, have a few drinks and we can talk.'

Pat said, 'No, no I'd rather not.' Talk? She wouldn't even know what to talk about, and surely wasn't going to talk about her difficult situation and why she was staying at her sister's, which anyway would take forever and a day to explain.

'Well,' he said, 'let's try – let me take you out at least for a nice meal.'

Moments passed in silence then she finally agreed. 'Where will I meet you? I don't drive!'

'Don't worry yourself, I'll come down and pick you up, we will go out and then I'll bring you home.'

Pat pondered the matter. No she thought she couldn't; her sister would never allow him to meet her from her house. So she said, 'Well I'm staying with my sister at the moment, I'm not sure if that will be all right, let me call you back.' Pat contemplated the idea of going out, is it really worth it? Having to get permission?

Pat walked sheepishly into the kitchen and asked Suzette, would it be OK if Chris could pick her up from her house to take her out. Expecting a sarcastic remark, that meant no, Suzette said, 'Yes that's fine Pat.' Pat was so shocked she nearly fell over.

'OK thank you,' she smiled.

She rang Chris back. She was beginning to feel a little excited. They agreed he would pick her up at 7.00pm that evening.

This then became a regular thing, Pat and her sister would go out on a Friday night, then on the Saturday, Suzette, Chris, his friend and Pat would all go out together. Things seemed to be going well, Pat started to look forward to her weekends out, until Chris' friend started not showing up on the Saturday night. Suzette, Pat could see was angry about this, but for a few more weeks Pat took the liberty of going out with Chris whilst waiting for things to turn sour.

Sure enough one Saturday Suzette turned to Pat and said, 'This is not working out.'

'What do you mean?' Pat asked.

'This whole arrangement, I'm not staying in on a Saturday

night, babysitting while you're going out!'

Pat replied, blurting everything out in one hit, 'But Chris picks me up, it's not my fault that your man doesn't show up.'

'Well it's not working for me, we will have to pick days, either you go out on the Friday, and I the Saturday or the other way round, either way I'm not bothered.'

Pat had arranged to go out with Chris that night as usual, but her sister said, 'No you're not going.'

'What do you mean I'm not going?' Pat asked.

'You're not going out! And you haven't even got a babysitter'

'But, but...'

'I'm not looking after your f****** children. While we're on the subject, let me just remind you, this is my house, and I do not want him picking you up from here anymore.'

'You have never had a problem before.' Pat said looking a bit confused.

'Well this is my house. I decide who comes in and who goes out.'

What could Pat say to that? Nothing! She went to ring Chris. Answering the phone he said immediately, '...I know, I know I'm running late, I won't be long hun...I will be with you in fifteen minutes...' And the phone went dead. S*** thought Pat ringing him back, what do I say now?'

'Listen Chris...

'Pat, I'm ten minutes away don't worry...' The phone went dead again.

Pat called him again. 'Chris I can't come,' she blurted.

'Oh – why what's wrong?'

'Ah...well, I think I have food poisoning, I've been feeling sick all day, I'm sorry.'

'OK, well... I'll get a bottle of wine and we can just spend the evening at yours.'

Knowing her sister was not in the best of moods, Pat said quickly, 'No, I don't think that will be such a good idea, I think what I really need is bed rest.'

'Well listen, I'm five minutes away now, and I really need to use the loo, and could kill for a coffee.' Pat, not knowing what else to say, agreed.

She approached Suzette. 'Listen um, Chris is just around the corner, he just wants to use the toilet quickly, and have a quick coffee.'

Suzette just snorted, 'No I don't think so!

'What? You won't even allow him to use the bathroom?'

'No!'

'OK, great, well I'm going to bed,' said Pat. Then bowing her head in shame she continued, 'When he turns up I suppose you will have no problem telling him you don't want him to come in, just to use the bathroom; as you never fail to remind me, it's your house and your front door.'

As Pat lay in bed, she heard a knock at the front door. She held her breath and squeezed her eyes shut, waiting anxiously for the shouting and the door to slam shut, but it didn't. She could hear voices. Had Suzette invited him in? No, surely not? Pat listened attentively; there was violence, abuse and lies definitely more than one person down there. She dashed round the room putting her clothes on and made her way downstairs.

In the living room there were candles lit and music playing in the background. A bottle of brandy was on the table and Chris was sat in the chair. She couldn't believe it, were her eyes deceiving her? Seeing her, Chris said softly, 'How are you feeling? Your sister said you were in bed, and the last time she checked on you, you were fast asleep.'

Pat was gobsmacked! How could she! At that moment Suzette walked in holding two glasses; she just glared at Pat in revulsion.

What have I done? Pat thought, except come downstairs to find this.

Suzette's poisonous mouth opened, her eyes staying fixed. 'Shouldn't you be in bed?' she snarled. 'Well, I suggest you find yourself back upstairs and back in bed.'

For the first time in her life, Pat actually ignored an order from her sister, and instead sat down quietly. Suzette then turned to Chris. 'Why on earth did you ask her to dance anyway? There were three sisters there that night, why did you choose her? Of all people, what did you see in her? It's not as if she is the most attractive out of the three of us, so what was it?' Her question was directed to him as if Pat wasn't there.

Chris replied, 'Well, to me Pat has the most beautiful eyes; they were like two beautiful diamonds dancing in the dark. So to me, she was the most attractive, not just out of you three sisters but also out of all the ladies in the club that night. I shouldn't have to tell you this, she is your sister, and I'm sure you're aware of her beauty.'

Pat wondered intensely: when Chris looked at her, who did he see – the same person she did when she looked in the mirror? And should she now give up trying to find out who exactly that person was?

At the time of writing, the scene just described took place over fifteen years ago. Chris and Pat remained friends, damn good friends; their relationship was always strictly platonic, like how a brother and sister should be. Pat attended his wedding and the christening of his first child. What a guy! Chris was a truly good friend, which he remains to this day, but with the new Pat now of course, Trisha. You know what they say; you can pick your friends but not your family. I'm sure if Pat had the choice – well need I say more?

But Suzette and Pat? Ah!!! She drove Pat to near insanity. This woman just wanted her blood. She just couldn't stand to see her happy even, as she knew, she always knew, that Pat had what it took to pick up the pieces of her broken life and move forward.

* * * * * *

I know it's not always as easy as it sounds but you just need to find your inner strength, get focused and motivated; set your goals, be determined, put the Lord in your prayers and allow him to do the rest.

Chapter Eight

Meltdown

So many memories, so much anguish … my heart is pounding in my chest, my palms are sweaty … I need a glass of water, maybe, a brandy even … I can hear the boys still playing in the garden with their water guns. Music is still playing and Isaac, Ilana, my Ricky and the friends we had over to help unpack boxes and black bags, are still bellowing above the reggae and soca music, all oblivious to what I am going through just a few feet away up in my shiny new bedroom.

I think: I can leave this right here, right now, I don't have to do this now, I can return to it another day. I try desperately to convince myself. But you know Trisha!! Strong-minded, strong-willed, never put off for tomorrow what you can do today, was my new philosophy. You can do this, I chant several times, as I lie back gently, and return in my mind to the past…

It was the final battle of this one-sided war that, we might say became the straw that broke the camel's back. As well as having to deal with her emotions, her feelings of failure and resentment, Pat still had a major practical hurdle to overcome, and that was her home. In terms of furniture, fixtures and fittings, if only she could somehow salvage what was still good, and replace what was essential, perhaps all would not be lost and she could move back in, have her own space again. She began visiting the property to inspect the damage yet again and try to assess her options. It was on her way back from one of these visits one day that she was so over whelmed with emotion and suddenly broke down in the taxi.

'Are you okay?' asked the concerned driver. 'What's the

matter? Why are you crying? Can I help you?' The poor guy didn't know what to do with her or what to say. Pat just kept crying, 'Talk to me,' he insisted, 'maybe I can help.'

Pat took her time and explained, through her tears and sobbing, about what had happened to her house, her children and how her sister was to blame for the fact that they were now homeless.

'Perhaps I can help?' said the driver again.

'How? How can anybody help me out of this situation?' said Pat, adding rather sarcastically, 'unless you've got a couple of thousand pounds to spare.'

As they pulled up round the corner from Suzette's house, the driver said, 'When are you next returning to your house?'

'I don't know,' said Pat, 'in the next couple of days maybe, I need to try and salvage some of our stuff there.'

'Call me when you're back in Maidstone and like I said, maybe I can help.'

Pat secretly met with the taxi driver on several occasions. He would pick her up from round the corner of Suzette's house and take her back and forth to Maidstone without charging her a penny. Could he have been another angel from God? On the fourth such occasion, on their way back he said, 'I have a surprise for you, don't be scared just bear with me, trust me.' He did a detour and we pulled up outside a house in Chatham. They both got out and were greeted at the door by a young, professional-looking female. Her name was Gina the taxi-driver's fiancé. They went inside Pat was offered tea, biscuits and fancy fairy cakes. All very pleasant, very nice, but Pat couldn't help but wonder, what am I doing here?

Then the taxi driver turned to her and said, 'I hope you don't mind that I have explained your situation to my fiancé? And we've been thinking, debating and checking our finances and we have what might be a solution to your problems. How do you feel about us buying your house in Maidstone from you?'

Pat was speechless. Then Gina said 'We've been looking for a house to buy and from what my partner said yours would be ideal. Think of it like killing two birds with one stone – we get the house of our dreams and you get the money to start a new life for you and your children.'

Well, she didn't need to say any more. 'Yes,' said Pat. 'Yes it's a deal.'

'I would like to see the house if that's okay with you?' Gina said. With that we all got swiftly in the car and headed to the house.

'I love it!' was Gina's reaction. 'It's great, fantastic, just what we wanted.'

The deal was done, and Pat returned to Suzette's with a smile on her face and a spring in her step. However she kept the arrangement under wraps, for she now knew the type of person Suzette was, and there was no way she was going to let her ruin this opportunity.

The weeks went by, Pat the taxi man and Gina met frequently at the house in Maidstone, engaged their own solicitors. They were set to exchange contracts and completion was within arm's reach. It was on their return to Suzette's house one evening that they were met by Suzette standing outside her front door. She was fuming, smoke almost bellowing from her ears and nose like a dragon.

'Where have you been?' she demanded. 'Who is that?'

'I don't know, um…he's just a taxi driver.'

'Don't lie to me! I'll ask you again, who is he?' But this time she didn't give Pat a chance to answer. 'I know he's been picking you up and bringing you back here for the last couple of weeks!' She leaned into the car. 'So, who are you? And how do you know her?' Pat introduced the taxi driver, who said simply, 'Hi' and drove hastily off. Some weeks passed and Pat was feeling slightly more confident, knowing that the house sale would be completed soon. One afternoon Suzette gave her some money. 'It's your turn to collect the boys from school today,' she said. 'And when you do I have promised them a treat at McDonald's on the way home; do it for me will you?' making it sound as if Pat had a choice.

'Yeah, sure,' answered Pat like the obedient child she was. Then Suzette added, 'Don't hurry back, let them take their time and enjoy their treat.'

Pat instantly forgot the arrangements for the taxi driver and his fiancé Gina to meet with her that afternoon. When she returned with the children some hours later she was welcomed by a very cheerful and excited Suzette who ushered her into the living room. To Pat's surprise there sat Gina and the taxi man. Trying to cover her embarrassment at forgetting their meeting and her shock of seeing them socialising with Suzette, Pat poured herself a drink and went over to join them. Gina stood up abruptly and turned to her fiancé. 'We're leaving,' she said, 'now. Please, let's go.'

Pat couldn't understand why they were going in such a hurry, as she had just got there. She apologised for not meeting them as arranged, but they were here now and she was here now, so what was the problem? What was going on?

'Don't leave, don't go,' said Pat. 'We still have a lot to talk about.' Gina didn't utter a word. The taxi man put his arms around her and they left. Suzette followed them to the door, whispering and smiling. Pat couldn't make out what they were saying. When they had left she said, 'Suzette, what was that about?' Suzette just laughed, went up to her bedroom and closed the door.

The following day Pat got to Chatham as quickly as she could and went directly to the taxi man and Gina's house. Anxiously waiting for an explanation, all she got was a door opening, then slamming shut in her face she knocked and knocked on the door, but it did not open again. She sat on the step and wept for quite some time. What have I done? She asked herself, why are they treating me like this?' Hours passed and still no one appeared. Then an unfamiliar car pulled up on the drive. 'Are you Pat O'Neil?' asked the driver, a man she had never seen before.

'Yes,' replied Pat.

'I'm only going to tell you this once. Leave here and don't come back!'

'But I need to speak to Gina and her fiancé, the taxi man,' protested Pat. Then there was another screech of brakes behind her. It was the new white Vauxhall Cavalier she had got to know so well, the taxi driver's car.

'What are you doing here Pat?' he asked her. 'What do you want? You have no right coming here, please leave, and leave now.'

'But why, what have I done? Why won't you talk to me?'

'Talk to you, are you taking the f******* p***? Get away from my house and don't come back! Go on f*** off.'

'But, but…'

'But what? Oh turn off the water works Pat, I don't know what you're crying for? I believed you. No, we believed you. We welcomed you into our home.'

'But…'

'We supported you.'

'But…'

'My Gina even helped you clean up the mess in the house. Now listen mate, you need to leave now, I'm getting p***** off now. So do yourself a favour and f*** off.'

Pat's mind was in disarray, in complete bewilderment she asked, 'What about the house, the sale?'

'What sale? There isn't going to be a sale you stupid cow!'

Twenty years later, as I revisit these memories I still do not know what was said and done, presumably by Suzette, to cause Gina and my taxi man to suddenly discard our friendship and dismiss our business arrangement.

In this latest annihilation of her hopes, in the confusion and distress at this act of wickedness, where people she had trusted and liked were wantonly, by some foul means turned against her, everything came to a head for Pat. She couldn't take any more; emotionally she was wrecked, physically she was shattered, and mentally she was drained. She was now in self-destruct mode. And it was poor innocent Isaac and Ilana that paid the price.

Confused, disorientated, and incoherent she miscalculated the repercussions of her actions, thinking that the world would be a better place without her. Over and again in her mind she said: I'm no good; I'm just no good. I'm a bad mother, a bad daughter; a bad sister and of course a bad partner, there is nothing good about me. They were right all along, for all these years they've been right. Can't do it, can't look after them. I can't even look after myself. I couldn't even look after our home, look what happened to that. The words 'they are better off without me' replayed over and over in her mind.

Pat recalled reading somewhere, 'If you love a bird hard enough, deep enough and long enough and then let it go, if it returns to you it's yours forever.' Pat loved her children more than anything in the world, they were her pulse that kept her heart beating, pumping; she knew that. Finally Isaac and Ilana would escape the grief and the horrors of what was their family.

So, in this state of mind, she had to let them go, and pray that one day they would come and look for her, find her, and she promised herself that if they did, she would never let them go again ever.

In full meltdown mode Pat lead her two beautiful children to the social services department with a note in their hand, left them there. There was no verbal communication between Pat and the children, no actual words spoken, but the look on Isaac's face said it all. The hardest thing Pat had ever had to do. She got on the next train to no-where. The final stop would be her final destination. In her self-destructive, one track, pessimistic mind, she recited the headlines of the next day's newspapers: 'Young black female found floating in the Thames.' It would all be over, Pats' final resting place a pauper's grave, no mourners, no flowers, no one to read a sermon or say prayers. No tears, no nothing.

Or perhaps they would never find her body. She would stay forever in a watery grave, alone and cold, as she had always been, for most of her life.

Waiting on the platform for a return train, her heart racing, and her mind working overtime: what have I done? What have I done! She couldn't do it; she couldn't leave Isaac and Ilana like this. By the time she got back to the social services office, the grave that she had just dug for herself was closing in around her; she couldn't believe what a huge can of worms she had just opened.

Already they had contacted her children's school, and the school had contacted their Aunty Suzette; the social worker assigned to their case had already called round and spoken to her. Oh no she was too late, beating herself up yet again, why didn't I just get up and go to the local housing office? Why didn't I get help? Surely there must have been someone I could have turned to. Pat's simplemindedness, her inability to trust her own self and her own thoughts, the programming that she received led her to believe that she was incapable of doing anything right, had led to this situation.

From the initial meeting at social services, Pat sensed straight away that the caseworker had been taken in by Suzette's lies and deceit, as anything Pat had to say he totally dismissed. Her many failed attempts of trying to explain, the reasons behind her actions; the house, the money, the family, the lies, the abuse, the failure and the humiliation all had Pat scraping the barrel for breath. Trying desperately, clawing her way out of the depths of hell that she had put herself in. Asking the Lord; send me an angel of mercy, rescue me and my children. But still she found herself slipping further and further into the raging fires of this bottomless pit.

Nevertheless, Suzette was given custody of Pat's children. Just trading on the fact that she was a trained registered nurse from the famous Guy's Hospital in London, had also told social services where she believed her sister needed to be: Pat now frantic to undo the wrong, was willing to do anything to get her children back; sign any paperwork, go anywhere, do whatever they asked of her.

'We only need to do a blood test, as your sister has said you haven't been very well lately.'

'So?'

'Well, you haven't been taking your medication. Have you?'

'Medication what medication?'

'Your sister has already told us that you stopped taking your tablets three days ago.'

'I'm fine – they're just iron tablets.'

With a roll of her eyes and a deep breath, in a patronising tone she said, 'Look love, I understand you're upset and probably a little confused from stopping your medication so abruptly, but let's get you well. I'll take you to the hospital; you'll have a blood test, just to make sure all is well. Then we will sort out the children, OK?'

'Then I'll get my kids back? I didn't mean it, I didn't want to leave them, I didn't want to give them up'

'Yeah sure, whatever you say, let's just get you to the hospital for these blood tests.'

Pat remembered, the waiting room, it was cold and clinical. The words mental health, jumped out from every sign, poster and pamphlet. Where was she? It was Joyce Green Psychiatric Unit, a mental institution. This wasn't supposed to happen, thought Pat, what happened to the blood test? Now, separated from her beloved children, she was among paranoid schizophrenics, manic-depressives and people on suicide watch, while her sister, with her violence, lies and abuse had won yet another battle in this horrific, one-sided war she had waged against her from childhood.

For seventy-two hours Pat did nothing but cry, scream and pine for her children. Presumably the nurses were immune to this type of behaviour, they saw it every day. Unless they get fed up of you of course! Which one member of staff did in fact, requesting for Pat to be sedated. It was at the hands of a very special, caring Trinidadian nurse who wasn't even assigned to her case, but had heard all the conversations among other members of staff about her, and decided to read her notes.

Filled with compassion and disbelief this good lady came to Pat and held her close as if she was one of her own. She turned Pat's face softly towards her, holding it gently in both hands, and looking her squarely in the eyes she said, 'They are going to sedate you, do you know what that means? It means you won't be leaving here, do you understand that? As soon as they give you that injection you won't be seeing your children again for a long time, they will lock you up, and section you under the mental health act, so you listen to me carefully. You need to stop this crying right now and show them who you really are, and what you're about. I will leave you with these words of wisdom; take comfort in them and draw strength from them, but whatever you do, never ever forget them. You are a strong, beautiful, intelligent, black woman. You have the capabilities to do so much where others have failed. You have the potential to succeed. You possess a spirit that is clean and pure of heart, you have the ability to make others stop, stand and listen. You can beat this, my child,' she said softly.

Sure enough Pat did exactly as she said. She listened carefully to what this angel had to say, smelt the sweet, comforting aroma of lavender, and grew calmer. The lady then explained to Pat that there would be people coming to assess her and her behaviour. 'So when you don't agree with what they are saying,' she advised, 'don't cry and throw a tantrum, explain your version of the events cool and calmly, maintain eye contact and you will get through it.' Again, sure enough, this was precisely what Pat did.

Three days after being admitted, she was discharged. Free to leave, free to go, but go where? She still had no home, no money, and no idea how to get her children back. Pat prayed: Father God, forgive them for they know not what they do, forgive me for I didn't know what I was doing.

Not having seen her children for three whole days, all she wanted now was to be close to them. Ronald collected her from the psychiatric unit and they went straight to Suzette's house. Ronald told Pat's children to pack their bags, as they were going with their mother and him.

Suzette had other ideas. 'You can't take them anywhere,' she said, 'they're in my custody.' Pat didn't give her a second look, just continued helping them pack their stuff. Her so-called sister then threatened to phone the police and social services again, at which point Ronald stepped in with, 'Fine – do it then.'

Social services duly arrived and Pat tried desperately to explain and convince them that the children would be safe and well looked after. They weren't having it. Pat and Ronald left Suzette's and returned to London without Pat's children.

With nowhere left to turn, Pat remembered Mum and Dad, now living on the beautiful island of Barbados. In a last ditch attempt to save her sanity and secure the future of her children she called her parents. 'Mum,' she begged, 'will you come to England and get Isaac and Ilana from Suzette?' After Ronald's explanation of what had happened and why the children were with Suzette, Pat had no doubt in her mind that her mum would be on the next plane to the UK, she was sure of it. She didn't stop to think, to analyse or to remember. Despite all the past disappointments, anxieties, betrayals, guilt, harm and self-harm that Pat had endured, she truly believed when it came to her children her mother would be there for them. But, just as history has a way of repeating itself, so it was with Pat's experiences. 'I'm not coming to England until Marianne's baby is due!'

Her mother's reaction thundered into Pats ears and reverberated agonisingly around her mind. She tried to comprehend what had just been said. 'But that's not for another four or five months,' she replied in disbelief. 'We need you now, the children need you.' Next Pat was hysterical, and promising that from now on she would be the daughter her mum had always wanted her to be; she would become a nurse, she would go to church, stop smoking, drinking, having sex, anything, please just come, come now!

Her pleas fell on deaf ears, only to be followed by words of comfort and relief from her dad, who simply took the phone and said, 'Calm down Pat, your mother and I will be there by the end of the week.'

The end of that week came, but brought neither her mum nor her dad. Pat supposed Suzette must have thought she had won the war, that the victory was hers. Or at least that she was doing Pat a favour, or at best her children a favour. Her master plan for Pat, it was quite obvious: destroy the bitch; destroy her children, by whatever means necessary. The knock-on effects of this plan would be, ultimately, to destroy her mother. Their mother. The woman Suzette believed left her behind in the Caribbean with her grandparents till she was eight years of age, where she was doted on, waited on hand and foot and treated like a princess. At eight this privileged upbringing changed when she came to the UK, where she was the eldest sibling and found she had to muck in and help raise her younger sisters.

But why take it out on Pat? Why was she the target of Suzette's anger? What made her so different from the other siblings? Why at every opportunity did Suzette feel she had to vent her emotional resentment, her dysfunctional attitude and the lack of stability in her own life onto Pat? Is it that she felt the bond she saw between Mum and Pat was in fact her entitlement? Did she feel that Pat had the underlying attention that she yearned for?

Rather than handing Pat's children back to her, Suzette made them pack their own simple belongings into black bags and sat them on her doorstep, closed the front door and called social services, informing them that she no longer wanted them.

After the deepest breath she had ever taken, Pat exhaled. She remembered all the adults in her life that had taught her to be afraid, afraid of them, and afraid of what they could do to her.

She recalled the pain of what they had done, and hadn't done. My precious babies, oh my God! What has she done to them she thought. It was only by the grace of God that she found strength.

It was only by his mercy that she was able to give her children something that she never had; unconditional love, acceptance, recognition and approval. But did she really love them? Did she really accept them? Recognise them? And approve of them for the persons they were? Yes, yes of course without a shadow of a doubt, she loved her children, for all their faults, warts and all. Admittedly, perhaps she hadn't really wanted them at the time of conception, but from the moment they had been born she had loved them, with all of her heart and soul.

They were to her, two exceptional, unique personalities that possessed the finest of qualities that Pat could love forever. She loved their beautiful little faces, their stunning features. The way Ilana would sing and dance and find the most inappropriate moment to sing her favourite song to her mummy, 'I Will Always Love You' by Whitney Houston. Pat loved the way Isaac always made her laugh he was such a little joker, with his sticky out ears like Will Smith and a sense of humour to match. They were her life.

How Pat survived the next however many months without her children, God only knew, going to and fro repeatedly from London to Kent, seeing the children only when their foster carers would allow her. Her worries were of course for both of them, but her chief concern lay with Isaac. He was older and could understand far more than Ilana, who was still just a baby and didn't really understand what was going on. Pat called on the Lord God many times, and felt his presence through the strength and support of Ronald. God kept her sane, and he kept her safe in the knowledge that her children would be returned to her one day, sooner rather than later.

Ronald assured her that the fostering was just a procedure that had to be gone through; part of the process being for Pat to re-establish a home back in Kent, in London, in Milton Keynes or wherever, for the children to return to. To this end, she and Ronald jumped on the case with her insurance people, badgering them constantly to get her claim sorted out quickly and efficiently. One afternoon, realising they hadn't heard from the company for a few weeks, Pat rang them. The response alarmed her.

'Miss O'Neil, we only spoke with you this morning; there hasn't been any progress since then.'

'No you didn't,' insisted Pat. 'I haven't spoken with you for a few weeks – this is why I am calling you now.' The gentleman continued, 'There is a note on your file confirming all the details that were given to you this morning.'

'No! I didn't call you this morning.'

'Someone did. Answering to your name, and giving your date of birth, they even requested that the cheque be made payable to your sister as you don't have a bank account.'

'What sister?'

'A Mrs Suzette Brown…'

'Stop, stop right there,' interrupted Pat. 'Is there any way that information on the case and the cheque can only be given to me in person?'

'Yes, but this would mean you have to come to the office and put some security in place.'

Ronald and Pat hit the M2 motorway heading for Maidstone, Pat with ID in her hand and a password in her head. Neither of them could believe that Suzette could stoop so low as impersonating her and stealing her insurance money, but then whom were they trying to fool? If she could physically harm Pat's children, put them in care, put her in a mental institution, what was it to take her money?

Later that month Pat decided to visit Milton Keynes to see Marianne. The day was filled with nothing but pleasantries; drinks flowing, music playing, fun and laughter, and real family bonding, was taking place. Pat was relaxed, happy to be around her sister and feel welcome. Strange, it felt so different to the last time she was there.

The evening was upon them when Steven, Marianne's partner and Godfather to Isaac, rose abruptly from his seat, towered over Marianne and said in a serious stern voice, 'Tell her!'

Pat looked at him, confused and puzzled. Then she looked at Marianne whose persona had changed to something she had never seen before; she actually looked scared, all the while trying to avoid eye contact with Pat.

'Tell her,' commanded Steven once more.

There was an outcry from Marianne. 'Why? I don't want to.'

What happened next happened fast. Steven grabbed Marianne by the scruff of her clothes and leaned in close.

'Tell her, or I will!'

It was only then that the whole disturbing plot was revealed to Pat. Marianne dried her tears and gave one of her Oscar award-winning performances in front of Steven, and confessed that both she and Suzette had been planning to take the money from Pat's insurance claim.

But this was one battle that neither Marianne, Suzette or anyone else was going to win. Pat's rapid visit to the insurance company with her ID had made sure of it, and the cheque arrived safely in her account a few weeks later. The infinitely better news was that she was allowed to have her children back once her house was in a fit state for them.

Returning there to Maidstone was no easy task for Pat. With all the tears she had cried, where she found more tears, she really didn't know. Ronald remained at her side and she continued to draw strength from him.

But this harmonious brother-sister twosome was not destined to last long, money being, as they say, the root of all evil. Despite the fact that Ronald knew Pat was on a tight budget and had a short time frame to get the house to a standard that would satisfy social services and thereby have her kids back, he now began to badger, pester and harass Pat for money. One day it would be, lend me fifty quid, the following day it would be borrow me two hundred, the next week, can you give me a thousand, and so it went on. It was never-ending. Still weak and off-balance, still yearning for acceptance and appreciation, Pat gave in to his every whim and whimper. Was this the reason why Ronald stayed by her side, just for the money? She had thought they were close.

Pat was finding it difficult to cope yet again and to add to her problems Mark had started his pathetic antics again, there were poison pen letters from Suzette, and prank calls from all and sundry. She couldn't handle it any longer. She asked Ronald, would life be any easer and happier if she were dead. He suggested that she and the children move in with him. 'I think it's for the best, don't you?'

So Pat and the kids were on the move again, bags packed and heading to London. The first few days at Ronald's were fine, they talked a lot about how they would apportion the house, who was allocated which room and how they would redecorate; light-hearted conversation, joking and laughing, staying up till two and three in the morning, talking about nothing in particular. Isaac and Ilana settled quickly and nicely in to yet another new school, fortunately they were raised in such a way that their coping mechanisms were very strong, and being young they were able to adapt to their changing circumstances. They started to feel comfortable and bonded as a family unit, just the way mother had instilled it in Pat's mind from an early age; that family comes first! Finally Pat began to feel that this was home and maybe, just maybe, all these family values were worth something.

It was one cold and wet winters evening, when Pat and the kids returned home from school, that they were met at the door by Isaac's turtle pattern duvet cover laying in a heap on the driveway. Ronald, with his current girlfriend, had decided this kind of family set-up was no longer what they wanted. Only three short weeks had passed and again the children and Pat were homeless.

It is amazing where one finds strength in times like these, and the people you least expect to be helpful are the ones that come through for you. For Pat right then, it was Nash Luck Property Management that proved a mine of information, and extremely helpful. They located and offered her a small flat on Howard Road, within hours of Pat delivering the application form. The place was far from great but they had been in worse. She did her best to make it home but it wasn't ideal; for the first time in their lives Isaac and Ilana were sharing a bedroom, so of course another move was felt inevitable.

Pat didn't see much of Ronald till she had moved to her second house courtesy of Nash Luck, in Boundary Road. Here he became a regular visitor. Pat's heart was heavy once again. She hadn't really forgiven him for putting the children and her out on the streets. To her it was like he felt his home was too good for them, but now her home was the only one he knew. Well, it was comfortable, it was clean, it was home.

The next few years Pat and the children spent living like travellers, moving from one place to another. Just as they got settled they would be uprooted again for one reason or another.

* * * * * *

Now, when, as Trisha I look back and think about these events, it was nothing more than running away from myself, that's what Pat did. I blamed my family for many of the bad things that happened to me in my life, all my failures, and shortcomings, disappointments and guilt. But there comes a time, that when faced with all these emotions, you must stop crying, stop wanting, stop needing to be someone you are not. And instead look at and embrace the person that you are. It was at this point that Pat desperately needed to reassess her life, her dreams, goals and ambitions, and set in motion a plan to succeed.

No one can save you from yourself, but yourself, no-one can and no-one will. Out of the clutter you will find simplicity, out of discord you will find harmony and in the middle of all of this is difficulty, but with this difficulty comes opportunity. Only we ourselves can walk our destined path. Be strong now, because things will get better, it might be hell and high water now but it can't rain for ever.

Chapter Nine

Meeting Mr Right

After talking on the phone they were finally going to meet, of course in Barbados. Full of excitement, the long awaited holiday that they all badly needed, was in sight.

Sara worked for Air-Tours flight centre and she'd sorted out the kids' and Pat's flights for the past year and a half. The two of them had become phone buddies and finally Pat was going to be able to put a face to the voice, to the person she had become very fond of. Sara was already a friend, someone she could call up and just have a chat with, just casual conversation without getting too deep if she didn't want to, a level of candour that was perfectly understood and accepted.

Pat's dad dropped her, excited and eager at Sara's hotel. They were going for a traditional Barbadian meal and then on to one of the island's hottest nightclubs. With so much to catch up on over dinner, the chatter was endless! 'How are the kids and your mum? And you how are you doing?' Before Pat could even answer, Sara continued, 'By the way, I have a friend that I think you would really like – well actually he's a friend of my boyfriend. A true Barbadian, I think you two will be well suited. I'm going to set you up on a blind date.'

'No! No! No!' Pat hastily replied. 'I'm not into blind dates.'

'OK, no problem, we will make it a foursome.'

'No! No! It's OK, I'm just here for a three-week relaxing holiday, I have no time for dates, blind dates, foursomes or anything of that nature. Thank you very much, but no thanks.'

Sara laughed. 'Come on Pat, he's really nice.'

Pat sighed and pondered for a moment.

'Come on, trust me, he's really, really nice.'

Finally, once again Pat's obedient nature got the better of her. 'OK!'

Sara sprang out of her chair with the fullest grin, beaming with excitement now. 'Great!' she enthused, 'we are meeting him tonight!'

Taking her seat at their reserved table at the Lucky Horse Shoe Bar and Restaurant with her ladylike manner, full of airs and graces and minding her Ps and Qs, Pat waited in nervous anticipation for the – according to Sara – really, really nice guy to arrive. She was sooooo not disappointed when he walked up to the table, and greeted Sara and her boyfriend. Her eyes scrutinised every inch of his tall (six foot three?) muscular frame. She tried ever so much to keep her composure; she couldn't dare let it slip that her first impression was hmm… Wow, not bad at all! Quickly she refocused to his face. Only then did it dawn on her that she knew him; that she had met him before. Wasn't he the prat that she had dismissed on the beach the previous year? Yes, he was! Oh my gosh! This wasn't gonna work, was it? …

Still she remained composed, and tried to overcome the memory of the spiteful tongue that she had unleashed on this unsuspecting hunk of a man. After a few drinks and polite conversation he turned to Pat and said, 'I remember you – you're the lady with the dirty mouth.'

'And what do you mean by that?' Pat answered swiftly.

'You love to swear. I don't appreciate women that behave like fishmongers' wives.

With raised eyebrows, Pat promptly responded, 'Firstly, I'm not your wife, secondly, you don't need to appreciate me, and finally I can behave like a fishmonger's wife if I feel like it!' She was shaking her head like a spoilt little girl, looking in his face, with hand on hip; assuming the position of someone well and truly fired up. She waited patiently for his reaction. He smiled then laughed. It was contagious. Sara half fell off her chair and her boyfriend ordered another round of drinks. The atmosphere had lightened and Pat felt comfortable.

In fact they went on to have the best date ever! They laughed and joked all night and into the wee small hours of the morning. Pat hadn't felt this alive in years. In the fraction of the time that this man had entered her life he had made her feel:

A. Like a woman
B. Human
C. Interesting
D. Sophisticated
E. Confident
F. Pretty
G. Sexy.

And the list went on, and on from A right to Z. This was a real man! Not someone who was after only one thing, but after everything, the whole package.

So much for fun and laughter; but what would happen if and when Pat would let him in, and allowed him to peel back the layers? Pat felt scared out of her wits at the thought of all the mess, all the emotional baggage he would find. Would it put him off? She was frightened, frightened of everything, even her own thoughts and feelings.

Pat and Ricky spent the best part of the next three weeks in each other's company. She was wined and dined and treated like a lady. She was on cloud nine! She had truly been swept of her feet. For the first time in Pat's life she had met a man that wanted her for her! He was kind and gentle and asked the appropriate questions at the appropriate time. Never did he force her to talk about things that she wasn't ready to disclose to him. Neither did he get upset when she didn't want to talk. He made it clear that he was happy just being in her company. Doubtless he could see that Pat was quite a troubled person, but he was willing to take the time, have the patience to offer her help and support, in whatever shape or fashion she needed. To show her that he was there for her. He moved her. Every day was an adventure – trips to the movies, nights out clubbing, and so introducing him to the children was a piece of cake, he was just 'Mummy's friend.'

Pat's holiday was coming to an end. She hardened her heart to the thought that what had occurred was just a holiday romance, and that nothing would ever come of it. Yet saying goodbye at the airport was more of an au revoir than a goodbye, as, since she visited Barbados regularly, she knew she would see him again. It was a strange feeling she got, just the mention of his name gave her goose bumps, and the sound of his voice gave her butterflies in her stomach. Was this yet another angel that the good Lord had sent her? What was his mission? What unexpected situation might arise, that would make him the fireman that carried her from the burning building? Would he even want to see her again? What about the children? Will he accept them; more to the point will they accept him? That was another question.

Pat couldn't wait to tell her sister Marianne all about this man called Ricky that she had met and how teenage-like she felt waiting by the phone for him to call – would he call? Again she would ask herself: did she really mean anything to him, or was she just another girl in his little black book? Pat had settled back in to her uneventful, standard life routine – of work, getting the children off to school, picking them up and going to her second job, picking them up again, putting them to bed. (I'm sure many of you can identify with me on that one!)

The phone rang, please not another double glazing salesman, but no it was him, calling her from Barbados. Trying not to sound too eager and desperate she remembered her ladylike composure and spoke with eloquence and control. Then he asked the question: are you missing me? Pat tried to say: no not really, as she tried frantically to push aside her true feelings. Instead she said softly, 'Yes of course I'm missing you. Are you missing me?' secretly hoping and praying she would get the answer that matched hers and her heart's longing. 'Yes I am.' Hearing these words, for a split second Pat felt weak at the knees. Then he asked, 'When are you coming back?'

'I don't know,' replied Pat. 'Soon I hope.' Finally the phone call ended, after what felt like an eternity of childish banter: you hang up, no, no you hang up – no you hang up….A few minutes later Pat found herself phoning Sara, asking her to book her on the next available flight to Barbados, which in fact was in six weeks. December; yes, great Pat thought, just in time to spend Christmas in Barbados.

Those six weeks seemed to drag on and on and on. While Pat was busy packing Christmas crackers lights and decorations, her mind and her heart was focused on one thing, the same questions that had been disturbing her night's sleep, causing her to daydream and lose her focus and concentration at work: does he really like me? Could this really be true?

Mid December arrived and Marianne and her daughter accompanied Pat, Isaac and Ilana to Barbados for the festive season. Pat must have bored her sister half to death during that eight hour flight with her one and only topic: RICKY! She wanted to surprise him so much with this visit. At the airport Marianne and Pat had their ritual of a Banks beer – Barbados home grown – and a fag before heading off to Mum's. No time to waste, bags down, a quick shower, a snack and they were off to the beach.

Pat sat and waited for Ricky to finish his shift as a water sports instructor. She and her sister Marianne laid back, rum and coke flowing, and eyeing up the local talent, giggling and giving each man marks out of ten as they passed by. And then at last there he was, strutting his stuff down the beach looking mighty fine in his white shorts and his white, tight fitted vest top. His black shiny skin glistened in the sunlight, his muscles protruding, protruding yep they sure were, (ladies you know what I mean) his entire physique perfect. Damn he really was fine!

Pat's heart began to race, but before she was able to jump up with excitement and delight to tell Marianne here comes Ricky, Marianne had pointed him out and said, 'Wow, check him out in his white shorts and white top, Oh My Gosh he's hot – he's mine for the rest of this holiday.' Stunned with indignation on one hand and proud on the other, Pat tried to tell her that was her Ricky. But so overexcited and eager was Marianne to let her presence be known, that she jumped out of her deckchair, grabbed her make-up bag, reapplied her lipstick, fixed her hair, pushed up her boobs and repeated, 'Yeah he's mine.'

Well Pat had no choice but to stop in her tracks and tell her, 'I'm sorry Marianne, that's Ricky.'

'No, it's not,' she replied. 'It can't be.' 'Yes it is.' Pat was trying hard not to annoy her further. 'Have you slept with him yet?'

'No,' replied Pat with a muddled expression.

'Well he's not yours then, is he' Staring Pat straight in the face, was the same spoilt brat arrogance that had driven her crazy for so many years. The attitude Marianne had always displayed; that she was so much better, and prettier and everything else than Pat. 'May the best chick win?' she said challengingly as Ricky drew nearer to them, the mister about to come between her and her sister – well, that yawning chasm had opened up years ago, without the intervention of any man. 'Look at me, and look at you,' crowed Pat's baby but no longer cute sister, 'no competition!!!'

If Pat could look in the mirror at that precise moment, she would have done – and perhaps even believed yet again the lie her sisters had fed her from such an early age; that she was ugly, simple and unwanted.

But if Marianne was right that day on the beach about the 'best chick' winning, then Pat looked likely to be that best chick. So far so good, and Pat was staying away from the mirror, and all the old conditioned thinking that went with it. Ricky was about to take her in his arms for the first time. They say romance can blossom anywhere, but hey, given a choice wouldn't most girls opt for a tropical island? And Barbados is one of the best. The long, quiet anxiety that Pat had experienced – that her long desired physical connection with this man of her dreams, would somehow kill the romance, crack the mould, spoil the illusion – was about to be tested. After a year and a half of travelling back and forth between the UK and Barbados, the long-awaited day had arrived.

Their evening began with a sumptuous candlelit dinner, Pat gazing at her man (he was really hers, wasn't he?), trying not to look nervous – and trying not to eat too much. But the wine, the food and the atmosphere were all perfect, and a stroll arm in arm along a secluded moonlit beach was the perfect conclusion to a perfect day. Or would have been, but of course it wasn't the conclusion and they both knew it. Why not leave it here, thought Pat, why risk spoiling this moment, this magic, this paradise…?

But the way she was feeling that night, her skin glowing from the day's summer sun as they walked beneath the Caribbean stars, the surf washing high over the warm sands, her body hot, in every sense…to hold back now? It was impossible.

Their first kiss was tender, gentle, exploring, their lips touching, brushing, moving in harmony, each waiting for and offering, the tentative, trembling signals to go further. As, by this silent mutual consent their mouths slowly opened, feeling their way into the moistness of one another, Pat felt something stir deep within her, something she had not felt since her first, clumsy adolescent encounters. Now that same rapture, that same, shattering excitement was rising in her again, only now, with a man, a real man, a man she loved and worshipped, that thrill returned to her a hundredfold.

The touch of his hands on her body was electrifying, the sight and smell and feel of his taut, athletic, flawless physique, sending tremors through her. As they lay down and he entered her with long slow strokes, the waves of ecstasy began pulsating through her. His lovemaking was slow, controlled, caressing yet passionate, bringing orgasm after unbelievable orgasm, her hands gripping the sheets as he massaged her secret pleasure domains ever deeper and more powerfully. As they climaxed finally together, Pat cried out: 'Yes, yes, yes!' There was nothing more to say. Yes, he was hers, and she his; no further words were needed. Their bodies and spirits at last enfolded, Pat and Ricky slept like twin angels that night, and likewise ever after.

So I guess the best chick did win. When one takes time to sit and reflect about one's life journey, it's easy to sweep under the carpet the things that make us sad, the things that have hurt us, and the things that we would prefer to forget. But in all honesty it's these things that make us the person that we are today. I believe that on reflection I have a certain amount of thanks to give to my siblings, as they showed me the person that I did not want to be.

Due to that I have been able to sustain a good and healthy marriage. I have been able to raise four healthy well-grounded beautiful children. I imagine this is what led to the element of jealousy that I have encountered throughout my married life. Again, you know the old saying: you can choose your friends but not your family. During my yearlong engagement to Ricky Marianne continued with her 'he's mine' antics. She made it quite clear that she wanted this man, with no holds barred; she pursued him, phone calls and letters, even going as far as telling me that he was only staying with me for the beer. (Little did she know, but he didn't drink beer.)

It was while we were in Barbados for the second Christmas with Marianne that I fell ill; an asthma attack that left me hospital bound for three days. Ricky was notified and came to my assistance immediately. On my return to Mum's he visited every morning before work, and every evening after work. He would carry me to the bathroom, assist me in brushing my hair and apply cream on my skin. Displaying his kind and caring nature, even when I felt better and was able to do for myself, still he would make a fuss and insist that I relax – he'd got it covered.

Following our engagement party which Marianne did not attend, surprise, surprise, she called demanding an explanation, 'Why are you marrying this man? Don't you know he doesn't really love you, he doesn't really care – you're just a ticket for him to a new life in England. He will take you for everything you have, your money, your sanity, your daughter even, if you're not careful.'

'I don't have anything,' I replied. I don't have any money, and you lot think I'm half-crazy anyway! As for my daughter, don't be so stupid, I know my daughter, I raised her, she's not like you lot besides she's only eight years old.'

As if that was not explanation enough for her she proceeded,

'Well just for the record, let me tell you, he's not as great and wonderful as you think he is, he is a bastard, just like the rest of them. Come on Pat, he's a man, and you know what men are like, if you're going to insist on marrying this man, I should let you know what you're in for. Remember while you were sick in Barbados with your asthma attack?

'Yeah.'

'Do you really think he was coming every day just to look after you? Well let me set you straight – while he played your Dr Zhivago behind your back he was fucking me. In fact we made a deal that I would allow him to be with you for one year, take what he could take, get what he could get, then fuck you off and come back to me. So what was it – voodoo, black magic, because for the life of me I can't understand why he would choose to stay with you and not with me.'

I couldn't understand and didn't want to believe any of the words coming out of her mouth. He wouldn't, he couldn't, would he? Could he? Well if that wasn't bad enough, in the days leading up to our wedding Karmen was around quite a lot. I had asked her only daughter to be one of my bridesmaids, and of course she happily accepted. What 8-year-old girl wouldn't? She wasn't the most helpful person to have around. Day after day, she would come round, sit around not even offering to help, plan or organise the last minute things that needed doing. The only interest she showed was offering to do my hair and makeup on my big day. Evening after evening she would sit at my dinner table enjoying a well-prepared meal courtesy of Ricky, look in my eyes, smile and say how lucky I was to have found such a wonderful man, what on earth, did he see in me? What on earth did I do to deserve such a great man like this? He cooks, cleans, he looks after Isaac and Ilana like they were his own. How the hell did I get him?

It was two days before our big day when Karman stayed quite late after dinner. Normally she would walk the five 5 or ten minutes from our house to hers, but as it was late, dark, and had a chill in the air, I suggested to Ricky to drop her home. Having my shower and settling into bed waiting for his return, an hour passed, two hours passed. My mind started working overtime: had there been an accident? And if not, then where is he? What's happened? Why isn't he back already? Finally I heard his keys turn in the door. He'd been gone four hours. My initial thought was to jump up and start screaming and shouting and cursing maybe, but no I remained calm and awaited his explanation. 'I'm sorry,' was the first thing he said. 'I'm really sorry. Sorry I know I shouldn't have stayed out so long, I know I shouldn't have listened. Listen Trisha would you understand, if I said, first nothing happened OK, but right now I don't want to talk about the things she said. I just want you to trust me enough to leave it till morning, right now I am tired, I'm upset and I need to get things straight in my mind.' I wanted to insist that he told me everything right there, right then but I could see by the look on his face he needed time, he needed space.

I didn't have to wait long; morning came round quickly, the bright June sun beaming through the window. I was handed a cup of coffee and a tray. 'Your breakfast babes, eat up I'll be back shortly.' I heard the front door close, and the start of the car. Where was he going now? What was he up to? I tried hard to eat the breakfast that he had prepared, but I couldn't, my stomach was a mess, my feelings, and my nerves all on edge, inside my head spinning. I waited patiently.

When he returned Ricky sat close to me on the edge of the bed, he held my hand and said, 'I want you to know, I need you to understand that I love you. You are my life, my soul and my future. There is nothing anyone can do or say that will ever change that. You are the only person that holds the power to destroy how I feel about you. I don't really want to go into what Karmen said last night, all you need to know, is that it has made no difference whatsoever to how I feel about you. We are getting married in less than twenty-four hours. Nothing has changed.'

Despite these loving words that assured me of his feelings, I still needed to know what my sister had said. I needed to understand better, what this man was dealing with in his head.

He continued, 'I know your sisters and your brothers, your mother your father have put you through enough, enough heartache, enough distress, it's just more of the same really, you don't need the details. I don't want you upset the day before our wedding OK?'

'I appreciate that,' I said softly, 'but I still would like to know.' Ricky took a deep breath, paused for a while and closed his eyes. 'When we pulled up outside her house I said goodbye, goodnight, see you tomorrow maybe, expecting her to get out the car, so I can watch her safely into her house, but no she didn't, she just sat there looking at me, staring at me, I kind of felt embarrassed.' She said to me 'Would you like to come in?' I said to her 'No, no thanks, that's okay.' She said 'I have a nice bottle of brandy indoors, I'm sure you can do with a drink after dealing with her all day.' But I told her 'No, no I'm fine thanks, 'We will see you tomorrow, well actually, I won't Trisha will, I'm out and about all day with the lads', but Trisha she just kept staring at me. We sat there in silence for a few seconds then she said, 'Oh Ricky, I feel so sorry for you, you really don't know what you're getting yourself into!' Trish, I was a bit confused when she said that, but I just told her, 'oh yes I do, I'm marrying the woman of my dreams.' She said to me, 'The woman of your dreams, um, that's what you think.' I told her I needed to get going, that you would be waiting up for me, but again she insisted that I come inside, that there are things she needed to tell me about you.'

I interrupted, 'Things about me?'

Ricky answered, 'Yeah, but I told her there's nothing you can tell me about Trisha I don't already know. 'Well babes, she started waffling on about so many different things and after a while I lost concentration and I switched off, I was so agitated, I didn't want to hear any more, to be honest I felt like driving back home and leaving her in the car, then she said it.'

'What? What did she say to you?'

'That you were a prostitute, a call girl.'

'A what – did you say a prostitute?

'I was so shocked I couldn't even speak, that was the last thing I was expecting – I just couldn't say anything, nothing at all. In actual fact I said, 'Is that it? I need to go now.' And I drove back here to our house and just sat outside for hours thinking, pondering not quite sure what to make of that conversation, but I knew I had to make a decision. With this new knowledge, I had to decide whether I was going to go ahead and marry you, or not, whether I was going to allow this revelation to shatter my illusions, of the beautiful picture I had painted of you. If it were true could I handle that fact, that my new wife was or is a prostitute, selling her body for money? The wife that had told me about her sexual encounters, how at one stage in her life she had used sex as a punishment to herself. The wife that had told me how sex up until she met me was not for her, that she had been celibate for near on three years, was this all lies? The fact that she didn't sleep with me during the first year or was it two years, was it because she was sleeping with what twenty, thirty or forty different men a day? And if it wasn't true I said to myself, then we just put it down to another wicked, evil display of your sisters' hatred and jealousy towards you.'

I closed my eyes, took a deep breath and asked him, 'So what's it to be? Do you believe her or not, do you want to stay or do you want to go?'

Ricky looked into my eyes and deep into my soul. He said, 'I am not even going to ask you if you were, or if you are or not – because I don't care. I don't care because I believe that a woman on her own with children, has to do whatever they have to do to survive, to keep a roof over their children's head, to keep food on the table, clothes on their back. So, if you were, yes it was a bit of a shock hearing it from your sister, and if you were it makes no difference to me. If you weren't and are not then that's fine, again it makes no difference to me, but your sister is a nasty piece of work. I trust you, I love you and I believe that if you feel there is anything in your past that you have not already told me about, then I understand that you have your reasons. But I know you, for all what you have been through and shared with me, I can't imagine that you wouldn't have told me this. I know some things are easier to talk about than others. But I believe and know that you trust me enough, you would have told me.'

When our wedding day arrived Karmen turned up to help me get ready, but half an hour late, expecting to be welcomed with open arms as per usual. Perhaps she thought Ricky wouldn't have had the balls to tell me. She swanned through our house as if butter wouldn't melt in her mouth. I couldn't believe it. Never mind all she had said, this woman still expected for me to allow her to do my hair and makeup. Did she really think I was that stupid? I wanted my future husband to see me as the beautiful queen that he always referred to me as, not the ugly troll that she would probably transform me into. My chief bridesmaid could sense the tension and stepped in and did a wonderful job. Neither Karmen nor her daughter attended the actual wedding.

Most weddings have the odd mishap. Like the bride turning up an hour late, while the groom is close to tears thinking he has been jilted at the altar, or the best man forgetting the rings then finding them in his top pocket. Or the photographer taking pictures without any film in the camera, but thank God its digital, or the cake you spent months deciding on falls off the table. Best of all is the bride returning from the bathroom with her dress tucked in her knickers exposing her lacy stockings and suspender belt, and giving all her male guests an eyeful of her groom's new assets. And no, I didn't.

In fact none of those disasters occurred. It was a beautiful day. The Lord sent the sun that smiled on us all day, a small gathering of thirty people that genuinely shared in the celebration of the uniting of our hearts. And Ricky and I, Trisha now, have just celebrated our tenth wedding anniversary by renewing our marriage vows on the paradise island of Barbados.

* * * * * *

In order for us to heal we must come to terms with everyone and everything in our lives. Accepting that there will be people that are jealous of you for whatever reasons, even though you may feel you have nothing to be jealous of. Accept it and move on. When I look back on my own journey, jealousy played a major role in all of my struggles, and life's episodes. Creating a safe haven for myself was the hardest part. But it is possible for I have achieved it.

> Serious sport has nothing to do with fair play. It is bound up with hatred, jealousy, boastfulness, disregard of all rules and sadistic pleasure in witnessing violence. In other words, it is war minus the shooting.
>
> George Orwell

My eldest brother Roger, two marriages later, and three children, is still not happy. Ronald, with five different baby mothers and ten children, is still not happy, Suzette, one failed marriage after just five years, two children who have not spoken to her in the last five years, currently with a partner who is almost twenty years her senior and still not happy. Karmen, with nine engagements but never actually getting to the church, two children just like Suzette who have not spoken to her in the last three to four years, no partner, never a husband, and still not happy. Marianne, one marriage that lasted seven months, two children fifteen years apart by different fathers, and still not happy. Last but not least is me, Trisha, one marriage, four children and happy as Larry. Who would have thought that of all my mother's children I would be the one that would turn life around?

I have had to transform my negative experiences into positive advantages. Learn from bad experiences to make better choices in the future, restructure my weaknesses into strengths and opportunities. By no means has this been an easy or straightforward journey, nevertheless it has been a journey that has placed me mentally and physically, in an environment where I am now surrounded by love, success, hope and faith.

Chapter Ten

The Death of Pat and the Birth of Trisha

Life is an opportunity, benefit from it.
Life is beauty, admire it.
Life is a dream, realize it.
Life is a challenge, meet it.
Life is a duty, complete it.
Life is a game, play it.
Life is a promise, fulfil it.
Life is sorrow, overcome it.
Life is a song, sing it.
Life is a struggle, accept it.
Life is a tragedy, confront it.
Life is an adventure, dare it.
Life is luck, make it,
Life is too precious, do not destroy it.
Life is life, fight for it.

Mother Teresa

You have to be different. Until this moment of realisation, I thought there was something wrong with being different; trying to be like everyone else, trying too hard to be loved by them, but I knew I was different. I would never say that I was better than my family but I knew I was different from them. My faith, attitude and perception of life, my way of thinking, my qualities, which had been suppressed for years, yearning to be released; my skills, abilities and talents not surfaced, all made me different.

The purpose of a personal healing process is to come to terms with your past, see your present for what it is, and plan for your success in the future. This can be achieved by understanding who you are, and where you're going. I had come full circle; I had dealt with my demons, and now needed to lay them to rest. I now understood why I had always felt like the proverbial black sheep of the family, so different from my sisters; I now understood why I never felt that love, that bond that you are supposed to have between sisters. This was why…

Dad said I was born like it. They had told him I would never walk, or that the possibilities were slim to none. Operation after operation, they broke and reset the bones, each time a different, major setback. So there I lay, on my mother's bed for the first three years of my life, not being able to play or interact with my sisters. Mother wrapped me up in cotton wool treating me like I was some fragile object, an ornament that you dusted off once in a while and admired from a distance. I suppose in her mind she was doing what she thought best, keeping me out of harm's way, and scolding anyone that came too close. Yes, born like it, he said, both my feet turned in at right angles. Several operations later, and an endless amount of time spent in physiotherapy, the bond between my siblings and I never really developed. Instead I watched them from a distance and yearned for the day that I would be a part of their games and laughter.

After nearly forty years of heartache, and living a life full of anxiety, it took my father his own near death experience before he could give me these answers I needed to complete the picture of my life. You can eat five portions of fruit and veg a day, and exercise regularly as Mum would insist he did, but healthy behaviour means very little if you smoke. Dad was a smoker, a serious smoker. So the message that 'smoking is bad for you' albeit an old one, Dad paid little attention to.

He started smoking at the tender age of nine, back then I guess, it was the done thing, to show your maturity, to fit in with your peers. Nothing much has changed then! Dad always said when we questioned him as youngsters, that smoking was cool and made him feel sexy. 'In my day,' he went on, 'it was even considered good for your health.' Anyway, the message seemed to be, if it was so bad for your health and so frowned upon by society do you really think people all over the world would be doing it? Come on now, everyone enjoys a good smoke, look, everyone on the telly even smokes, all the great movie stars, no one could be seen acting in a movie without a lit cigarette in their hand, and what about the sportsmen and women they promote smoking with all their advertising contracts worldwide. So Dad sat back and enjoyed his sixty to seventy cigarettes a day, taking one to light the other and of course accompanied by a quick swig of neat brandy.

Dad and I had always enjoyed a funny, complex strange relationship. I remember when I was between seventeen and nineteen maybe, those days I consider as Dad's and my heydays, our good days, the great days. These were the days when Dad and I would party and rave at his regular haunts, confusing the onlookers as to whether I was his bit on the side or his extremely young wife; never for a moment did they guess I was simply his daughter. We would party the night away, in perfect sync, the dance routines of yesteryear that he had taught me were perfectly executed, so graceful, so expressive.

Elegantly nimble on his feet Dad was the true professional dancer and I was a mere student.

And I had always felt a special connection with my dad. Perhaps to me he had always said the right thing at the right time throughout my life. Even as I now realise it was perhaps just to calm the situation and to help me refocus, but whatever it was I was grateful for it. So when Dad started to constantly complain of pain and Mum quietly ushered him off to the hospital, on his return three days later it was quite a shock to my system. I didn't recognise the man who was standing before me. He looked like my dad and sounded like my dad, but there was something different, something major had changed. And it must have been a wake-up call to his soul, because this is when he chose to tell me about how it had been for me as very young child – the operations, being kept apart from my siblings. Why my parents had kept it a secret for so long I guess I will never fully know. Secrets, they say all families have them.

I vaguely remember back when I was sixteen, at an audition for Goldsmiths University Dance Academy, The Laban Centre, they noticed I had some medical defect that they considered as a disability, and asked me if I had ever had problems with my legs? Knowing nothing at the time I replied with a firm no. They then suggested (or was it requested?), that my lower legs and feet be broken and reset. I didn't mind, not if it meant I would get into one of the world's top dance schools. But Mum kicked up a fuss, and closed the discussion with an off the cuff statement which I didn't pay any attention to or even understand: 'You should be grateful that you can walk, never mind kick up your foot dancing; now you want to go and break those feet…?' kissing her teeth 'Chaa!' which meant, 'yeah, right.'

So, the understated truth was that I was different to my family, and finally I knew and accepted that there's nothing wrong with that. But that former, wrong and wronged self, Pat, had to be left behind, and she needed a proper burial. Trisha needed to be born. Pat had suffered and carried a lot of emotional baggage around with her all her life. This crap, for want of a better word, needed to be buried. I needed closure, and realised that all my efforts to change would be in vain unless that happened. For me it wasn't enough to just forgive or surrender. I needed a concrete demonstration that it was over, that my life and everything about it up until the day I changed my name and my nature, and accepted with grace all my personal differences, was completely closed.

The sea had a wonderful way of calling to Pat, its vast open density, the sun setting behind it, the colours of red and orange across the night sky, they drew her intensely. In fact she always thought should come to an end at sea, or in water somewhere, so where better a place could there be, for the perfect burial of Pat than a watery grave. While stepping out into Pat's final resting place I said a prayer, and told Pat what I was planning to do, and not to be scared. The prayer ran thus:

> Dear Pat
> I say this prayer to you, to thank you for all you have been to me. I thank you for all you have been in my life and for the many ways in which you have served me. We have had many great times together, and while our relationship was healthy and purposeful at one time, I find that it no longer serves me. It no longer supports what I desire in my life, or the purpose I believe God intends for me.
>
> Now I forgive you totally and unconditionally for any and all conscious and unconscious thoughts, words, and

actions committed by you that have had an unloving, unsupportive, unhealthy impact on my life. I now ask for and claim your forgiveness, for any and all conscious and unconscious thoughts, words, and actions of mine that have held you back from the truth, or any condition of fear, anger, resentment, guilt, shame or any other unhealthy emotion, you found yourself in, due to my inability to say no. You are now free to pursue your higher and greater good, and I am now free to pursue my higher and greater good. I wish for you love, light, peace, and an abundance of every good thing in God's kingdom.

I release you. I surrender the energy of you in my being to the presence of the Holy Spirit, and ask that you and any memory of you be transformed to provide productive and valuable energy according to God's perfect plan.

I love you Pat. I bless you. Trisha.

As the waves washed over my body and engulfed my face and head I knew I had brought Pat's life to a close. I was overwhelmed, by an immediate feeling of calm and peace.

This was rudely interrupted by coughing and spluttering. I heard voices saying, 'She's lucky to be alive…she's lucky to be alive…has anyone called for an ambulance…?'

Did I nearly drown? Slowly I opened my eyes. So many strangers, so many people there for me, worried about me. But for me it was the start of a new life. I didn't need an ambulance, I didn't need anything or anyone, only to embrace the new me, Trisha, Trisha. It had such a beautiful ring to it,

'We're taking you to the hospital,' a voice from the crowd said. Without shouting, screaming or crying, calmly I said, 'No, no thank you it's okay I'll be okay.' Then I recalled the very recent moment when I had realised that the undercurrent had begun sweeping me out to sea. Realisation, but not panic no; let the Lord's work be done I had thought. As I bobbed up and down and swallowed half the Caribbean Ocean, peace and tranquillity bathed me. I didn't want to die, I had a whole new life ahead of me, but the current was strong and I couldn't swim!

I will always thank them and thank God for his mercy that they fished me out and brought me to shore. I walked calmly down the beach for the remainder of the day, I watched the Lord's beautiful sunset. I listened to the birds sing their good night lullabies. I observed closely the outstanding magnificence of the waves, of the sea. Glory be, Lord God the Almighty, I thank you.

Through you all things are possible; you have never forsaken me, where mankind has failed me, you stayed by my side. You gave me the strength and cleared a path of righteousness for me to follow. When I was weak and unable to proceed you carried me, for this I am eternally grateful. I know this is the start of a new journey, and where it will take me, only you know. But I am willing, now able and fully equipped to do your work.

While reading this book you will have noticed numerous references to my faith, and the goodness of the Lord, and his help in time of trouble. Allow me to take you now on a brief journey, an express trip if you like, covering the long and winding road to faith which I have taken throughout the years.

To begin with, the O'Neal's were raised within the Catholic faith. From an early age I was taken to church and attended Bible studies. As a child I was sent to a Catholic school and we were all baptised as Roman Catholics during our childhood. I made my first Holy Communion aged ten and Confirmation at fifteen. Mum was a firm believer, and wanted to instil that belief in her offspring.

Christianity is the most practised religion in the world, estimated to have over two billion adherents. We were led to believe that Jesus was the Messiah promised in the Old Testament, that he was the son of God. His father sent him to earth where he suffered and died on the Cross and on the third day rose from the dead. This was to save humanity from their sins. There are three main elements to God in Christianity, the Holy Trinity - God the Father, the Son, and the Holy Ghost. This wonderful, frightening, inspiring story, and the worldwide doctrine which sprang from it, settled deep within my subconscious.

But as I grew and became curious, I began to learn about and explore other religious ideas and beliefs.

Working on a project for my CSE Religious Education exam at age sixteen, I stumbled across the Rastafarian movement. Rastafari is a relatively new, Africa-focused religion, which emerged in Jamaica in the 1930s following the coronation of Haile Selassie I as King of Ethiopia. Rastafarians believe that Haile Selassie I is God, and that he will return to Africa the descendants of those black people living in what is regarded as exile through colonisation and the slave trade. The theology was based on the ideas of Marcus Garvey, a political activist who sought to improve the status of his fellow black men.

The Rastafarian movement spread like wildfire, raising awareness across the globe, in large part through the popularity of reggae music and one of its most talented and successful international practitioners, Jamaican singer-songwriter Bob Marley, whose music and teachings inspired thousands. (1945–1981) During my exploration of Rastafari I witness some of its ceremonies and rituals, including dancing, drumming, meditating and the inhalation of marijuana. These practices are thought to increase spiritual awareness, and reach a state of heightened consciousness. Feasts of natural produce, fruits and vegetables are laid on, though meat is refrained from, especially pork, which is believed unclean. Alcohol is also avoided. I listened attentively to the lessons of the Rastafarian elders, the belief in reincarnation, and that life is eternal.

It was my two elder brothers Roger and Ronald, who brought home Islam, professing they were now devoted Muslims, following the knowledge and beliefs that Islam began in Arabia and was revealed to humanity by the Prophet Muhammad, and they called God Allah. They told us about the key tenets of Islam: the belief in Angels, in the holy books, the prophets Adam, Ibrahim (Abraham), Musa (Moses), Dawud (David), Isa (Jesus), the belief in Muhammad (peace be upon him, the final prophet), the belief in the day of judgement, the day when the life of every human being will be assessed to decide whether they go to heaven or hell, belief in predestination, that Allah has the knowledge of all what will happen, as Muslims they also believed that this doesn't stop human beings making free choices. It was fascinating, so different – the culture, the clothes, the whole thing.

Then I studied Spiritualism, inspired by my visions. Spiritualists claim to communicate with the spirits of the dead. They believe in a continued future existence, and that people who have passed on to the spirit world can and do communicate with us. This communication is thought to be beneficial to the dead and the living. The modern Spiritualist movement dates from 1848 when the Fox sisters of Hydesville, New York produced knocking sounds purported to be messages from a spirit.

Spirits are said to communicate through those with special skills, called mediums. In the 19th Century such events, in public or private, were referred to as a séance, whilst nowadays mediums practice at Spiritualist church services or in private sittings. The spirit communication can be verbal messages, or physical manifestations such as tapping. The validity of Spiritualism has always been controversial, partly because of the negative image given by fraudsters. Spiritualism differs from most other World religions in not having the same kind of institutionalised set up, or body of theology.

I don't even remember how I came across Paganism; Wiccans, Druids, Shaman, Sacred Ecologists, Odinists and Heathens all make up this diverse collection of believers. Some of these groups concentrate on specific traditions and practices such as ecology, witchcraft, Celtic traditions and worship certain gods, but most pagans share an ecological vision that comes from a belief in the organic vitality and spirituality of the natural world. Best to clarify though what pagans are not: they are not sexual deviants, they do not worship the devil, and they are not evil. They do not practice so called black magic, and their rituals do not involve the harming of people or animals.

I guess after all my encounters with these varied religions and beliefs I chose not to stay with one, but tried to be empowered by all of them. I chose to take from Christianity and Islam the belief in one God the most high; I call him Jah. From Spiritualism I am ready to believe that those who have passed on can communicate with us. From the ecological vision of the pagans, I accept the spirituality of the natural world. I can't say that I hold one religion in greater esteem than another. I have simply, I hope, learned something from each. I like to call it Trisha's religion, which is not meant to sound pompous.

As regards the Rastafarian movement, my appearance might prompt the notion of an allegiance here. I do like to refer to the lion that represents Haile Selassie I, known as the 'Conquering Lion of Judah' – the symbol of Rastafari, and talk of my hair as my lioness mane. Rastafarians are forbidden to cut their hair, and I have allowed mine to grow and twisted it into dreadlocks. Maybe it's more a fashion statement, as it is for many, but perhaps it's something more. The Rastafarian colours are red, green and gold, and sometimes also black. The Red signifies the blood of those killed for the cause of the black community throughout Jamaican history. Green represents Jamaica's lush vegetation and the hope for new growth and the eradication of oppression Gold symbolises the wealth of Ethiopia, and Black the skin of the Africans who initiated Rastafari. Rastafari is not a highly organized religion, but a movement and an ideology. Many Rastas say it is not a religion at all, but a Way of Life, and encourage one another to find faith and inspiration within themselves.

Back on that beach…Ricky was the first person I told of my experience that day. He held me close and whispered, 'You are the most beautiful woman I have ever met, you're unique, strong and gifted, I believe when you say you'll be okay, you really will be okay.'

Love the life you live,
Live the life you love

Bob Marley

Most people think,
Great God will come from the skies,
Take away everything and make everybody feel high.
But if you know what life is worth, you will look for yours on earth:
And now you see the light,
You stand up for your rights. jah!

Bob Marley

In a nutshell it was Brother Lincoln, a boyfriend of one of my house mates from way back when, who was also one of Isaac's godparents that over the years helped me to put into perspective my beliefs – the belief in the reality of mythology, the supernatural and spirituality, the combination of many segments, of different faiths that have so much meaning to me.

Ricky's soothing words and genuine gestures moved me yet again. Trisha was born, and though filled with mixed emotions she was strong and knew exactly what she wanted, when she wanted it, and how she wanted it. I believed this was love, love that I never experienced before. My mind was made up; here in his arms was where I wanted to be, now and forever. For love will take your breath away – true love, when you really experience it. Made by the Holy Spirit it will rattle your brain and melt your heart. I know because it happened to me. My dearest God had sent me yet another angel

Finally the tears dried, and the memories began to fade. I had come full circle, dealt with my demons and was ready to move on. On reflection this healing process is not one to be taken lightly. If taken seriously and given the time, it can serve you well. I truly believe that this healing process can be used as a guide, to confront and overcome your demons, whether they are family, friends, work matters, addictions – drugs, alcohol or smoking. By looking closely at the trauma these demons may have caused you in your life, taking a positive attitude and a willingness to change, accepting the ability to cry when need be, you have the capability to stop beating yourself up for situations you have no control over and are not responsible for. This way, you can acknowledge that you are unique, special and worthy of love and you deserve peace and respect.

* * * * * *

A gentle kiss wakes me from my slumber.

'Honey I've brought you up something to eat and a nice cold drink. Are you okay? I checked on you while you were sleeping, but I could see you had been…' 'Shush, it's okay I'm okay.' I interrupt quietly, before he can finish his sentence.

He nods sweetly, he understands what I was trying to say, but continued with, 'I'm so proud of you, you have worked really hard to make all this possible, but babes, please don't overdo it in your condition, you know you need to rest and take it easy at times OK?'

'Are the boys still playing water fights? And Isaac and Ilana – what are they up to?

'The boys are fine, they're still in the garden the whole place is soaked. But them all right still – they're having fun. Isaac and Ilana are cleaning up. Girl, you've done such a good job with those two, I'm so proud to see the way they get along, thank God they didn't take after your side of family.'

'Well to be honest with you, there were times throughout their lives that I thought that they would. I know sometimes it must have been difficult for the both of them, but God is so good that when they were at their most vulnerable he shielded and protected them. I suppose getting through the hard times made them strong, not just as individuals, but strengthened their brother-sisterly relationship.'

I suppose when we have children, and we're going through difficulties and dealing with demons, it scares us half to death to think about or even consider what it does to our children. So we hide, we turn a blind eye and we hope for the best, this is not always the best way to deal with what our children are going through. But if this has been the path that you have chosen, like myself you need to heal, you need to confront those negative feelings of failure towards your children, cry and let it out, let the tears flow, allow them to surface from the well of your soul, from the depths of your heart, and erupt, bringing with them all the anger, all the fear, all the s*** that you have suppressed for whatever period of time. Then celebrate with love, hugs and kisses and at times explanations and acknowledgements.

Look at my son, look at my daughter, specimens of perfectly rounded, educated, young, intelligent, focused, loving, kind, driven people. The list is endless. My son was a lot older at the time of my great difficulties; perhaps he felt the stress, the burdens and the pressures of what I was going through. Maybe more so than my daughter; she was a lot younger and perhaps might have been more protected in terms of the Holy Spirit. Isaac was more my confidante, my springboard, that I could go to and try to unload some of my worries and concerns – not really taking into account at the time, what effect it may have on him in later days. But I am proud of him nevertheless, I do believe he's mature and he's strong, even if maybe a little confused when it comes to really understanding proper family values.

Isaac was around six or seven years old when what I call the major issues occurred in my life, especially when they were placed in care and I was carted off to the mental institution. I believe that Isaac has great recollection of these traumatic times. I use the word traumatic because as a six-year-old being left at the social services office by his mum, with a note in his hand, the only stable, consistent, reliable person in his life, I think calling it a trauma is an understatement. I know for sure he witnessed a phone call I made to my parents while they were in Barbados and the outcome of that phone call stayed with him for many years, perhaps even to this day, which possibly accounts for the breakdown of the relationship between him and his Grandmother. I don't blame him for this; these are the things that I wanted to protect him from.

I do believe and feel very positive that I have installed good family values in all of my children, that they understand that family members are meant to be there for each other, with no hidden agendas, that they are supposed to love each other unconditionally, they are supposed to accept each other for who they are, what they are and believe in, and what they stand for, regardless of whether it meets with your approval or not.

But they also know that they are not doormats not for anyone, you do not turn the other cheek and allow people to take liberties with you just because they are your brother or your sister. They also know, never to be afraid and never to go out of their way to seek approval from anyone. I believe they know that approval comes from within and as long as you celebrate who you are, what you are and where you're going, you can stand tall, and be strong, conquer any obstacle, and win any war.

I believe there is a very strong bond between my two older children, Isaac and Ilana, that they have mastered unconditional love between each other. I further believe there is no circumstance or situation that either one of them could find them selves in, where they couldn't go to the other and seek comfort. I think they both know, and I'm very proud to say this with a big smile on my face, not to take the p***.

You know, I do believe I am truly blessed, that we are truly blessed, and when I say we, I mean every one of the six members of this family. My Ricky walked into my life at a time when I was down and out, but he proved himself not only to be a good husband to me but also a wonderful father to my first two children. When I look at Ilana's face when she is talking and joking around with him, it's amazing, nobody would ever know that he is not her biological father. He is her father in every sense of the word, a daddy that she loves and treasures dearly. The relationship between the two of them, from the very start has been magical. Simply because of the way she took to him, like a duck to water, I pray every day that the bond between them never change. She loves Ricky profoundly and I'm very proud of that fact.

I know that for Isaac it was a little different. When Ricky came into our lives Isaac was the man of the house and had been for many years. So for him, it was a little more difficult to accept another male in the home. But yet again, I'm proud of him and I'm proud of the way he handled the situation. The way Ricky made him feel, that he is his first son, heir to his kingdom, and that has never changed. Despite the fact that we have had two children within our marriage, two sons, Isaac is still Ricky's eldest, his number one. And I love him for that. I love the way he and Isaac interact, there are times when he would usher me up to bed, so that he can have male bonding time with his first son. It's wonderful. So again, I pray and ask the Lord to keep it that way. Don't ever let it change.

'To tell you the truth, Isaac and Ilana are great kids. Just look at the way they deal with Rhys and Ryan.'

'I know.' I replied.

'Do you remember the day when Rhys was born? Ilana was so excited and Isaac didn't know what to do with himself, but they were great. Ilana the surrogate mother.'

'Yeah, we've always said if she ever ill-treats them the world would know about it, they are that close. And boy do they love their Isaac. I just can't wait to see when they get big, and my three boys dressed up going out partying together, or just chilling, relaxing and enjoying each other's company. I am one proud mum.'

Don't get me wrong yes they have their moments like all other brothers and sisters but nothing as compared to me and mine. Throughout the years I have cried many tears for myself and for various members of the family and of course for my children. What I discovered though was that the most painful tears come from your inability to tell your story. I was once told this, by a very wise fourteen year old (who looked very much like me) 'Tell your story mum, it will help to heal you and maybe even heal someone else.'

By me telling my story, and you perhaps telling yours, it will aid, even enable whatever healing process is required. If I am truly to heal, and maybe help others in the process, I must tell parts of that story that I am uncomfortable with, and find forgiveness Not because I am different, special or unique, but because I have been blessed to be able to cry myself through to a day and a time when joyful tears flow abundantly from my heart and allow me to stand strong. This flowing from the heart can bring you to a new perspective and a new understanding, to celebrate yourself, your healing and your journey through that process. Telling my story, gives me something to celebrate, likewise I hope you will find reasons to celebrate too. The moral behind the red coat at the beginning of this book is, well, we all know the story of Little Red Riding Hood; she was kind, caring and always willing to do for others. These were the words that my mother told me when she bought me my first red coat for my eighth birthday. Those words, and the thoughts and emotions that went with them, have stayed with me throughout my entire life.

But now the red coat has many more meanings: the colour red, not only is it my favourite, but it symbolises love, pain, strength and power. The coat itself symbolises your ability to perceive what lies beneath. To perceive the truth, like a blanket of snow that always manages to find the darkest parts of the world and give it light.

The combination is who I am today. Today Trisha is as strong, perceptive and effective as she can be in her world. I hope I still reflect the kindness, the love and the willingness to help others that Little Red Riding Hood did.

So, here we are. Ricky and I together in our empty room, surrounded by our boxes, black bags and huge storage containers, the trinkets of our dreams jingling within, reminding us of where we have been, and where we're going, whispering their presence and a future we have yet to experience.

Forgiveness
Anyone can hold a grudge, but it takes a person with character to forgive. When you forgive you release yourself from a painful burden. Forgiveness doesn't mean that whatever happened is OK, and it doesn't mean that that person should stay and be welcomed in your life.

It just means that you have made peace with the pain, and are ready to let go.
www.Happiness in your life.com

'Well, these boxes won't unpack themselves,' smiles Ricky. I sigh peacefully, and return his smile. 'I wonder if we'll ever find homes for all these beautiful things.'

Ricky holds up the mirror, hammer in hand. 'Where would you like this darling?'

Seeing his reflection next to mine, I smile. My Victorian mirror needs a special place where I can see her and she can see me. Ricky hammers in the nail and I carefully offer her pride of place. A mirror is relevant, why? I hear you asking yet again – more on that later.

When I consciously stop and stare at myself, my reflection in the mirror, the person I see now no longer becomes distorted or dissolved. It is my reflection, one that I am proud of, and delighted to see.

When I look at that face, that person, I am happy to ask the question: 'Trisha – is this really you?'

Without warning I grab Ricky's arm, hold on tight, trying to balance myself on him. Realising what is happening, he lets go of the mirror. This pain just won't quit. It's like a constant drilling of a safe room door. It's hurting my eyes, shattering the side of my face, travelling down, where will it stop? Oh no! Here we go again.

Please feel free to leave your comments or ask me any questions on the website below or send me an email for a more in-depth chat.

Website: www.talleyne-is-this-really-you.com
Email: isthisreallyyou@Outlook.com

SD - #0010 - 070726 - C0 - 198/129/9 - PB - 9781780355849 - Gloss Lamination